LASTING
LOVE

To Tom & Tatiana,

May you always know the
joy of lasting love.

[signature]

Phil. 1:6

HOW TO
AVOID
MARITAL
FAILURE

LASTING
LOVE

ALISTAIR
BEGG

MOODY PRESS
CHICAGO

© 1997 by
ALISTAIR BEGG

ISBN: 0-8024-3405-3

1 3 5 7 9 10 8 6 4 2

Printed in the United States of America

To Susan,
who from
lane to lane
remains the
love of my life

(Are you going to church tonight?)

CONTENTS

Foreword	9
Acknowledgments	11
Introduction: What More Can Be Said About Marriage?	13
1. When Marriage Doesn't Go According to Plan	23
2. Before We Say "I Do"	37
3. Sealed with a Vow	71
4. The Role of a Wife	99
5. The Role of a Husband	137
6. Pulling Weeds	175
7. Planting Hedges	207
Conclusion	227
Notes	239
Study Guide for Spouse and Group Discussion	243

FOREWORD

When flames of romance are hot, the shared love leaps high and radiates warmth to everyone close at hand. The excitement and devotion may appear to be permanent, but often the fervent promises simply do not hold up under the tedium of everyday life: ardor cools, ashes form. It is a picture of far too many marriages.

Divorce statistics in America fluctuate around 50 percent, but much higher is the rate of disillusioned husbands and wives who struggle with apathy; the fire is gone. At some desperate point they seek marital advice from a minister. Whereas the sparkle of passionate love once glowed in their eyes, now a sobering discontent clouds their faces. The story of what happened to their dream and the hope that happiness can be regained energizes the pages of *Lasting Love*. It is the pulse beat of a pastor's heart, the distilled wisdom of years devoted to romance recovery.

Alistair Begg stands at a determinative crossroads for many married couples. Senior pastor, counselor, man of God, he is far more than a pat-answer man. I am privileged to call him my friend and colleague. His therapy? A return to the original model for marriage, a reminder of the only anchor strong enough to hold in twentieth-century storms. Alistair teaches the art of a lasting relationship. He calls each partner to bury self-interests and diligently tend the fire of his or her own home hearth. After fifty years of marriage to my own Jeanne, I give witness to the validity of his remedies.

Our chilly world of self-indulgence easily smothers tender caring; but endearment can be reignited, assures Alistair. Such a word of encouragement not only soothes the soul, but rescues and rebuilds broken relationships. Here is a book to be given serious attention, to be discussed, and to be practiced. The glad results are guaranteed.

HOWARD G. HENDRICKS
DISTINGUISHED PROFESSOR AND CHAIRMAN
CENTER FOR CHRISTIAN LEADERSHIP
DALLAS THEOLOGICAL SEMINARY

ACKNOWLEDGMENTS

In reading this book, it will quickly become apparent that I am greatly indebted to many people for their help. This I freely acknowledge.

- Those who have taught me about marriage from their pulpits and their pens
- Friends and family, who are living illustrations of the biblical principles which follow
- My Parkside Church family for their continued loving support
- Greg, Jim, Anne, and the others at Moody—they were never moody!
- My friends at Camp of the Woods, New York, and Maranatha, Michigan, for allowing me to practice on them

- Ed and Mona Atsinger, James and Suzanne Karls and Paul and Betsy Seegott, who provided lovely places in which to write in peace
- Hank and Helen Craig for "watching out for me" and teaching me how to eat "southern"
- My secretary, Kay Roberts, for all the typing, research, coffee, and friendship
- And most of all Susan, Cameron, Michelle, and Emily, who know the worst about me and love me just the same

Soli Deo Gloria

WHAT MORE CAN BE SAID ABOUT MARRIAGE?

"Another book on marriage?"

Those are my sentiments exactly. If ever there has been a surfeit of material generated on any one subject, it surely must be this one. It seems everyone has something to say about love, marriage, and commitment.

Consequently, one would expect that by now our homes would be classic illustrations of marital contentment, excitement, and abiding faithfulness. Yet sadly, that is not the case. In fact, the extent of confused thinking and subsequent chaotic living is staggering.

So what's wrong? Are all those books being purchased and left unread? Do we read them, but not apply what we have discovered? Do we lack the will to do the hard work necessary to rise above marital mediocrity?

I suspect that the problem is much deeper. The fundamental problem is not, as we have been led to believe, one of interpersonal disintegration. At an even deeper level is a theological issue that remains unaddressed. We have spent the past quarter of a century focusing on ourselves, and we are currently adrift on the tides of pragmatism and psychological theory. In the matter of ethics, we are attracted to teachers who will pander to our own desires. No longer willing to listen to the truth, we have begun to wander off in pursuit of man-made fictions.

Despite the fact that we feel a desperate need to drop anchor, we remain unclear or, worse still, unconvinced about the location of a safe haven. Yet it is well past time for the harbor lights to be turned on and for us to heed the wisdom of the harbor master.

In surveying the vast array of books on relationships within the family and particularly on marriage, there is much that is helpful—very helpful. However, the issue is usually approached from one of two ways. Occasionally the books have a strong biblical base, yet they frequently contain little practical application. Far more books have an extensive practical and experiential perspective, but at the expense of establishing a sufficient biblical foundation.

This book is my humble attempt to close the gap by beginning with theological foundations and then building levels of practical application on the strength of the underlying material. This is also an attempt at preventive medicine. It is written primarily for those who are contemplating marriage from the vantage point of singleness, who are in the early stages of married life, or who have enjoyed a number of years of marital bliss and are tempted to conclude that this kind of material is interesting but undoubtedly irrelevant. However, it may also prove helpful to those who are already dealing with the effects of decay.

I am writing from the perspective of someone who has enjoyed twenty-two years of happy marriage—loving, learning, sharing, and growing. Yet my wife and I have seen far too many couples similar to ourselves whose marriages dissolved after a long and apparently healthy start. We are unwilling to feel it is ever safe to assume, like so many others do, that *it will never happen to us!*

Every pastor has a collection of sad tales related to this topic. Here's one example shared by H. Norman Wright about a professional man describing his gradually increasing involvement with a young woman.

A new woman came to work in our office. We struck up an acquaintance and began to talk each day over coffee. In time she began to share the problems in her own marriage and we found that we were both in a position of drifting away from our spouses. We actually found that we communicated better together than with our own spouses. We looked for reasons to be together—we shared similar interests and hobbies. I had no ulterior motives—no sinister plans—but I enjoyed our time together as friends. We saw each other every day for a few moments, and once a week we went to lunch. In time I began to compare Elaine with my wife. I saw so many positives in Elaine. The more I compared, the more defects I saw in my wife. Then one day it hit me. "I was in love with another woman. Me! No! I'm a married man with three children. I'm chairman of our church board. This happens to others—why me! Why did I let myself get into this mess?" I felt confused. My work suffered—my relationships suffered. I tried to stop my involvement. Some weeks I didn't see Elaine that much. Other weeks I saw her every day. I had to! I had to! "Last week it happened. We made love. I am so torn up right now! What do I do?"[1]

In some cases contemporary society is willing to admit to knowing nothing and starting fresh with the basics. This is evidenced in the success of the "_____ for Dummies" book series, which deals with such issues as computer technology, chess, and classical music. In a sense, this book is, unashamedly, "Marriage for Dummies." It is a refresher course on the basics, and hopefully you will find it to be much more.

You've heard the statistics: One-half of all new marriages will end in divorce. This marriage malaise shows no signs of passing. If you haven't experienced it yourself, perhaps you've suffered through it with a friend or family member.

It would be one thing if we learned from our mistakes. But among those who have been divorced, the chances for survival in a second marriage are even worse. Those who marry three times face an 82 percent failure rate. A new label has even been established for such people: *serial monogamist.*

The median age for divorce is now twenty-eight. Indeed, broken marriages and single parent families are no longer social stigmas. How did we arrive at this sorry state of affairs?

Twenty years ago, therapist Carl Rogers wrote a landmark book, *Becoming Partners: Marriage and Its Alternatives.* In it he offered this assessment:

> To me it seems that we are living in an important and uncertain age, and the institution of marriage is most assuredly in an uncertain state. If 50–75 percent of Ford or General Motors cars fell apart within the early part of their lifetimes as automobiles, drastic steps would be taken. We have no such well organized way of dealing with our social institutions, so

people are groping, more or less blindly, to find alternatives to marriage (which is less than 50 percent successful). Living together without marriage, living in communes, extensive childcare centers, serial monogamy (with one divorce after another), the women's liberation movement to establish the woman as a person in her own right, new divorce laws which do away with the concept of guilt—these are all gropings toward some new form of man-woman relationship for the future. It would take a bolder man than I to predict what will emerge.[2]

Rogers was describing what he saw as the great potential for some new form of man-woman relationship in the future. Writing from the perspective of a humanistic unbeliever, his assumption was that we were socially evolving from the outdated concept of marriage to a whole new improved system. A quarter of a century later we look out on the wasteland of marital disintegration.

Even the most liberal sociologists now confirm that our entire culture is in disarray. The courts wrestle with the issue of homosexual marriage and grant parenting privileges to same-sex couples. As illegitimacy (remember that word?) reaches 90 percent in urban areas and sexually transmitted disease continues to spread, anyone who raises a voice in protest is regarded as an out-of-touch dinosaur, or worse still, as part of a bigoted reactionary remnant of the Dark Ages.

There is no other way to say it: The picture is bleak and the prospects dim. Tragically, Christians are part of the fallout. Christian marriages are falling apart at virtually the same rate as those of the secular world. Too many believers succumb to the devil's lies and are better acquainted with social fads and self-help theory than with what the Bible has to say about marriage.

When the devil approached Eve in the garden, he insinuated that God didn't really mean it when He said that death would result from disobedience. Satan's strategy remains consistent: "Look around, men; it's almost the twenty-first century! Do you really think God wants you to be an old-fashioned husband? Such ideas were for ancient times, but you don't really think He means it for you!" With such supernatural propaganda, how are we to prevent ourselves from becoming part of the sorry statistics of failure and disintegration?

One clue comes from a recent newspaper I saw. Most newspapers have pages of photographs of bright-faced young couples proudly announcing their engagements and another section filled with the portraits of those celebrating anniversaries. But what was striking in this particular paper was that the anniversary photo of a couple celebrating fifty or more years of marriage was paired with the couple's original wedding photo. In most cases the two photographs were side by side.

It was a most encouraging few pages that prompted me to ask: "How did they do it?" These couples surely discovered somewhere along the journey that they needed to have realistic expectations of what was involved in loving each other throughout their lives. They must have learned to pay careful attention to the basics.

This struck me recently as I finished a biography of one of the greatest strikers of a golf ball, ever. Ben Hogan was consumed with a passionate longing to do everything correctly. His desire bordered on an obsession that frustrated him and made others around him unhappy. Then, he tells us,

> in 1946 my attitude suddenly changed. . . . I would guess what lay behind my new confidence was this: I had stopped trying to do a great many things perfectly because it had become clear in my mind that this ambitious overthoroughness was neither possible or advisable, nor even necessary. . . . ALL THAT IS REALLY REQUIRED TO PLAY GOOD GOLF IS TO EXECUTE PROPERLY A RELATIVELY SMALL NUMBER OF TRUE FUNDAMENTAL MOVEMENTS.[3]

As I observed those older couples and pondered their recipes for success, the more I realized that although marriage is not exactly easy, it is straightforward. And as I talk with older couples, they confirm that in each successful marriage there is a commitment to do the basics well most of the time.

In the chapters that follow, I hope you will discover "a relatively small number of true fundamental movements" that will make your marriage more consistent. Perhaps you can learn to avoid many of the pitfalls that destroy so many others. And even if it's too late to undo some of the pains or consequences of your past, it's never too late to learn to face the future with a commitment to the God through whom all things are possible and a firm resolve to do better from now on.

This book contains a number of case studies adapted and/or compiled from numerous counseling sessions and real-life situations. You may see yourself in some of the problems that are presented. But if all goes well, you'll also see yourself in the "success stories" of those who overcame initial problems.

Let's begin by taking a look at some marriages that were not what they should be, followed by insights from the Bible on what marriage *ought* to be.

CHAPTER ONE

WHEN MARRIAGE DOESN'T GO ACCORDING TO PLAN

Karen waved good-bye to her husband and kids. As she closed the garage door, she added yet another item to the "to do" list in her mind: call the Genie service man. It wouldn't be long until that noisy, vibrating door refused to work at all.

She walked through the laundry room, ignoring the perpetually growing stacks of white and colored clothing. Coffee first and then she would climb those mountains.

She had been up since six o'clock, but this was the first moment she had had to herself. Even though the twins were high school seniors and could fend for themselves, they had grown to expect Mom's packed lunches, which were far superior to cafeteria food. Dave also depended on her. His shirts and dry cleaning, needed for another four-day business trip, were ready for him.

The routine was automatic after so many years of practice. In the early days, she would drive Dave to the airport, often with the twins still in their pajamas. The three of them would be back on Friday evening, awaiting the return of the conquering hero and hoping he had enough energy left to talk, listen, buy them ice cream after dinner, and take them to the park to push them on the swings.

These days, though, Dave left the car in Park and Fly. If he could catch the early flight on Fridays, he would usually drive directly to the golf club. Karen knew he needed the "space" those nine holes provided, yet she secretly wished it was more like old times. He was a good provider, didn't miss the school conferences, and certainly hadn't developed one of those potbellies like many of her friends' husbands.

It had been a while since romance caused her heart to race and her breath to become short, but there was a lot to be said for good old faithfulness. She knew imagination had never been Dave's strong suit, and predictability was better than nothing. Still, it would be fun just once to . . . She suspended her wishful thoughts and reheated her coffee in the microwave. If only it were that simple to put the warmth back into their marriage.

Dave seldom boarded his flight until the last minute. He was on the phone as usual. "If we wrap things up by, say, two o'clock, I'm sure we can get in eighteen holes before dark." As he spoke he smiled at his traveling companion, who was finishing her first Evian of the morning. When his company hired a woman as the marketing director for his territory, her responsibilities had originally been fulfilled from the home office. But for the past year she had begun to travel with him at least twice a month.

She was eleven years his junior, and at first he felt a sense of brotherly protection for her, especially when he saw the stares she attracted from other men. But over time he had developed an attraction to her. He couldn't remember exactly when it happened—perhaps the morning they were jammed together in the back of an over-crowded 727 en route to San Antonio, pressing their knees together as they attempted to keep their lunches from sliding off the foldout trays into their laps. He could not deny the sensation he felt that day, unsure whether he was imagining that she felt it too.

But by now he was looking forward to his trips with her. She was someone to talk to who had a life beyond laundry and lunches and home-making. He had begun to compare and contrast Karen with his colleague, and although he had not fallen off the cliff, he fully realized just how close he was getting to the edge. And with every inch his anticipation mounted.

※ ※ ※

From all outward appearances, Jack and Cathy were the ideal couple. They had been friends since childhood. Their families vacationed together. They were like brother and sister in high school, and only in college realized the depth of the feelings they had for each other. Neither could bear to think of spending the rest of a lifetime absent the companionship of the other. Everyone seemed delighted when they married.

The first twenty years of marriage went as expected: two healthy children (Danny and Carla), coping with the challenges of schools and business, and eventually a cottage on the lake. Cathy and the kids would move to the lake as soon as school was out, and Jack would join them on weekends and for three weeks in August.

One summer Carla was away at school, so Cathy suggested they rent her room to a college life-guard named Rick. Jack was impressed with Rick —the firmness of his handshake, the way he would look you in the eye, and his winning personality. He immediately considered Rick a candidate for a sales position in his company. Danny also got along well with Rick, and they went sailing together many evenings when the pool closed and Rick got off work. Rick had a knack for getting things done. He would form a plan and follow it through.

Yet, eventually, Danny started to get a strange unsettling feeling about Rick. It began one night when he awoke in the middle of the night and heard voices on the porch. He picked up snippets of conversation through the screen door. He heard his mom saying, "I haven't always felt that way. There used to be a lot more excitement." The responding voice was Rick's: "When did things begin to change?"

"What's this? A midnight feast?" Danny interrupted, trying to disguise his sense of internal disquiet with joviality.

"Oh, no," said his mom. "Rick and I just started talking about everything. We must wrap it up, but I haven't had such a good conversation for some time."

When Danny awoke the following morning, Rick was already at the pool. *Probably was nothing,* he thought as he looked at his mother. She was forty-five and aging well—very well, in fact. She seemed to be improving with age. Her daily routine of running with their golden retriever and her discipline with the abdominizer allowed her to face *Shape* magazine at the grocery checkout without any feelings of inadequacy. Danny's college buddies frequently told him that his mom was "hot," and they joked about how his portly, balding dad had attracted her.

"He didn't always look like that," Danny would tell them. "He just kind of let things go."

The next weekend when Jack arrived at the cottage, he was greeted by a sleepy stare from their faithful retriever.

"Hello!" Cathy's voice sounded a bit odd as she came from the other room to give him a kiss on the cheek. "How was the traffic?" she asked. "Would you like some spaghetti?" "Did your father reach you at the office?"

As Jack began to answer her questions one by one, he thought he detected a kind of flush about Cathy's face and neck. He knew she hadn't been running because the dog was in his usual spot in front of the wicker rocker.

"I've been helping Rick tidy the pool," she volunteered. "He works so hard and those lounge chairs are such a hassle to wipe off and straighten. Nobody seems to have a care. They just walk away and leave him to clean everything up."

"That's what he's paid for," growled Jack, surprising even himself by the tone of his response. He couldn't put his finger on any one thing, but by the time he left on Sunday evening, he was sure there was something strange going on with his wife. Was this a physical change in Cathy? Or something else?

His fearful suspicions intensified on Monday when he received a call from his longtime friend, Henry, who owned a cottage across the lake from his. Henry wanted to have lunch with him, and they set it up. Jack wondered what was so important, since they had spent part of the previous day together.

Jack was in his usual booth when Henry arrived. Henry wasted no time as he leaned forward and fixed his gaze on his dear friend. "Jack, I do not know how else to approach this, so I'll just come straight out and say it. Helen and I have strong reason to believe that Cathy and the summer lifeguard are developing a relationship that is destructive and wrong." He then went into details that ripped a gaping hole in Jack's emotions which Jack could neither cover nor control. His shoulders heaved under the weight of the news. Somewhere in the distance he could hear Henry assuring him that he and Helen would do everything they could.

DANGER SIGNALS

These two fictitious stories emerge from count-less conversations I have had with couples who failed to recognize the danger signals and plunged head-long into disaster. Usually they arrive dreadfully embarrassed and reluctant to unfold their story. But most of their comments are things I've heard numerous times before:

- "We never thought it would happen to us."
- "How can God allow such things?"
- "We probably were never right for each other."
- "Why didn't someone say or do some-thing?"

And the list continues. Sadly, in the majority of cases the couples do not work out their prob-lems and stay together. They fail to put in the effort necessary to climb the mountain of forgive-ness and restoration, choosing instead to settle in the plain. And from my observation, the plain is overcrowded with tents.

THE ORIGINAL PLAN

After a husband and wife confront problems of the magnitude of those described in these opening stories, they are quick to see that their marriage hasn't gone according to plan. Yet they aren't always so quick to identify exactly what that plan is. Each of the partners usually has some idea of what he or she expects, yet frequently those expectations aren't clearly expressed to the other person.

The original plan of marriage was God's idea. Marriage is of divine origin. It is not, as many young people choose to believe, an institution that human beings dreamed up. If it were, then of course it could be revamped or even set aside. It is therefore imperative that we begin by understanding and submitting ourselves to what the Bible teaches concerning the origin of marriage. At the same time it is vital that we understand the purposes for which God has ordained marriage.

In the preamble to the wedding ceremony, it is usual to hear these purposes stated succinctly. Marriage was created for the lifelong help and comfort which husband and wife ought to give to each other. It exists for the well-being of family life so that children, who are gifts from God, might be brought up in the instruction of the Lord. Marriage strengthens human society, which remains healthy only when the marriage bond is held in honor.

When God created Adam, He said that it was not good for him to be alone. God made Eve as a human complement and partner for Adam. It is immediately apparent that humans were created to be social and sexual beings. God's blueprint for marriage calls for an exclusive relationship between one man and one woman as they enter into a lifetime covenant. The concept of a *covenant* is vastly different from a contractual agreement that may be set aside at the whim of either party. When God entered into a covenant with Abraham, the solemnity of it was emphasized with a "thick and dreadful darkness" (Genesis 15:12) and a number of animal sacrifices (15:9–11, 17). The covenant promises were made under the pain of death.

Similarly, marriage, says Jay Adams, is a "covenant of companionship."

> Marriage involves a covenantal agreement to meet all of your spouse's needs for companionship (on every level: sexual, social, spiritual, etc.) for the rest of your life. It is, therefore, a final act. Christians, unlike non-Christians today who enter into trial marriages, annual, renewable marriage contracts, and the like, need not live daily under the threat of divorce. The binding nature of the divine covenant assures them that divorce is not an option. That is a wonderful difference that Christians possess. The covenant is a life commitment.[1]

In marriage, a man and woman are joined in a way that cannot compare with any other relationship. It is not a tenuous arrangement that may be forsaken at will. Rather, it is a binding commitment involving the legal, physical, emotional, and spiritual dimensions of becoming one.

Despite the clarity with which the Bible speaks to this matter, many Christians appear to be confused. Recent surveys reveal that as many as two-thirds of those interviewed considered divorce "a reasonable solution to a problem marriage."[2]

While we may not be surprised by such a perspective among non-Christians, it is tragic to consider the extent to which the salt has lost its taste when it comes to sexual purity and marital fidelity in the Christian community. If we are going to be at all successful in avoiding marital failure, it is imperative that we exercise our minds in the truth of Scripture and yield our wills in submission to God's clear directives.

Our submission to God's design must be total and wholehearted—whether we can see the pragmatic benefits or not. For example, in an environment riddled with sexually transmitted diseases it is not difficult to commit to the ideal of monogamy. People may care little about the divine mandate, yet they consider the human benefit. If we adopt this approach, we will only do as we are told when we are able to identify our immediate rewards. So if wives do not see the benefits of submitting to their husbands, they will seek loopholes through which they can escape the obligation instead of submitting to the truth of Scripture. God's Word is to be obeyed whether we find it to be immediately to our liking or not. It is in becoming obedient to His Word and His will that we discover true freedom. Consider the benefits:

- Making a lifelong commitment focuses our attention on "staying the course" rather than on short bursts of enthusiasm.
- The freedom of marriage "in the Lord" is similarly rewarding. To be able to share with one another at the deepest levels of spiritual understanding is a great joy.
- As husband and wife learn to put each other first, they discover the pleasures that come only when they get past living for themselves. Wives are challenged to "submit to your husbands" (Ephesians 5:22) and husbands are told to "love your wives, just as Christ loved the church" (Ephesians 5:25).

  If these intense obligations are defined in purely negative terms, they may seem deplorable. But seen from God's perspective, these commands provide order and joy in a relationship. Attempting to continually put oneself first never works. But learning to put a spouse first can become a lifelong pleasure for those with hearts for God's Word.

- Rejecting divorce as an option allows for great security in marriage. It means that when problems arise—no matter how great those problems may be—the couple will learn to return to the instruction manual of God's Word and rely upon the help of God's Spirit.

Some time ago in my *Tabletalk* daily Bible reading program, I found the following comments to be most helpful.

In their commitment to the unity of marriage, the couple promises to be faithful to each other if poverty and disease should come upon them. They vow before God and man to be faithful if they meet a more attractive, a more intelligent, a more compassionate person. The wife vows to be faithful if her husband loses his high-paying job, his esteem before men, his mental faculties, or his youthful vigor. She commits to him even when he doesn't measure up to the standard God has set for him, even when he does not love her as Christ loves the church. The husband vows to be faithful if his wife loses her beauty, her charm, or her tenderness. His commitment remains steadfast even when she is unsubmissive, disrespectful, and unable to manage the household well. Through it all, the two remain one flesh.[3]

Without an underlying covenantal commitment between marriage partners, it is too easy to find "deal breakers" that will negate the marriage contract. So, since the covenant is so important, we need to take a closer look at exactly what it is that marriage partners agree to do.

CHAPTER TWO

BEFORE
WE SAY "I DO"

Most of this book is for those who have already embarked upon the journey, those who have, as we say, "tied the knot." So this chapter is for those who haven't reached that stage. You are in the single world, which is filled with opportunities and fraught with dangers. You are aware that the decisions you make today contribute to the person you will be tomorrow. The number of disintegrating marriages causes you to wonder whether it is advisable to even consider it. And, besides, you have a number of projects to complete, plans to fulfill, and journeys to take before you reach the settling-down stage. At the same time, you would like to have clearly in your mind a strategy for relationships that will prevent you from making unwise decisions and living with regret, and which will allow you to consider the possibility of meeting your partner for life somewhere along the journey. So let me try to help.

DOES MY RELATIONSHIP TO GOD COME FIRST?

When we think about relationships, we should be very clear that our relationship to God must come first. We may well have to pause immediately and ask ourselves just where we stand when it comes to this aspect of our lives. Have we entered through the narrow gate, taken up our cross, and begun to follow Jesus? Or are we simply being kept afloat by the faith of our family? Are we seeking first the kingdom of God and endeavoring to do the right thing, or are we just living to please ourselves? Until we settle this matter, we are unprepared to make the right decisions about other relationships.

We must also recognize that our significance and fulfillment in life is not to be determined by whether or not we have a relationship with someone of the opposite sex. You will know of sad stories involving friends who rushed into relationships driven by fear of what others would say about them if they were not "dating" or "involved." Settle the matter right now. There is no good thing which the Lord will withhold from those whose walk is blameless. There is no need for panic. It is He who makes everything beautiful in His time. To be unattached to someone of the opposite sex may be God's best for you now and perhaps always.

TO MARRY OR NOT TO MARRY?

Of all the choices that we ever make, there is little question that the decision about whether to marry and then whom to marry is as crucial as any we will face. When we consider the desire to avoid marital failure, is it fair to say that one way to do just that is to opt for singleness? In order to answer that question adequately, we must pay careful attention to what the Bible teaches about the single state. This is a subject that is highly relevant and, for many, emotionally charged.

When Paul addresses it in 1 Corinthians 7, he sets this question in the larger scheme of things. Eternal verities control his response to practicalities. The present scheme of things is passing away and, consequently, he says, all of our contact with the world should be as light as possible. So, while we are to be involved in the world, we are not to be engrossed in it. A vibrant Christian faith changes the way in which we view all the elements of life.

39

MATERIAL POSSESSIONS

So, for example, when it comes to possessions, our concerns about our bank balance should not outweigh our interest in making deposits in the bank of heaven. When we buy "stuff" we should not hold on to it tenaciously but, rather, treat it as if it really isn't ours to keep.

THE PURSUIT OF HAPPINESS

Our culture is preoccupied with whatever makes us feel good. While there is certainly no virtue in feeling bad or being morose as an alternative, the believer has a different perspective. When our gaze is on eternity and when spiritual victory means much, then the happiness that results from personal success, promotion, or financial gain dims in comparison.

DEALING WITH DEATH

Christian faith does not remove us from the experience of pain and loss and tears. But when we lose a loved one, we realize that it is only for a while and that we will be reunited. So we do not fall apart and lose our motivation for life, for we have a living hope and a vital purpose.

THE IMPACT OF ETERNITY

Paul does not develop any of these areas; he

merely summarizes them to show the impact of eternity in these most practical areas, not least of all, as we shall see, the question of relationships. "There is no time to indulge in sorrow, no time for enjoying our joys; those who buy have no time to enjoy their possessions, and indeed their every contact with the world must be as light as possible, for the present scheme of things is rapidly passing away" (1 Corinthians 7:30–31, PHILLIPS).

Now it is in this wider context that he says: "From now on those who have wives should live as if they had none" (1 Corinthians 7:29). What does this mean? Paul is clearly not contradicting his earlier teaching, in which he stresses the importance of husbands and wives working hard to fulfill their obligations to each other. His emphasis is surely this: Marriage, in all its demands and benefits, should not be allowed to reduce the believer's obligation to the Lord and His work. The apostle is not about to allow us to use the responsibilities of marriage (and, we might add, family) as excuses for slackness in the service of the Lord Jesus. This teaching challenges the contemporary lists of priorities with which we have grown familiar and undoubtedly comfortable. The list is usually given as follows:

God

Family

The Lord's work/church

Work

Leisure

But what does item one really mean for most of us? It is number one on every believer's list, but what does it mean in practical terms? Does the fact that we may have neglected elements of family life in pursuit of the Lord's work justify the shrines that we have built to the family at the expense of corporate worship and fellowship and evangelism? It sounds so right to talk about being a family-centered church until we pause and realize that our only focus is to be God Himself. We must try and come to a realistic understanding and application of the words of Jesus, which frankly turn a great deal of our comfortable preoccupations on their heads: "If anyone comes to me and does not hate his father and mother, his wife and children, his brothers and sisters—yes, even his own life—he cannot be my disciple" (Luke 14:26).

Consider the extent to which the cause of the Gospel is impacted negatively on account of our unwillingness to take Jesus at His word. Is it not true to say that, in the interests of "family," increasing numbers absent themselves from the privileges and obligations of worship on the Lord's Day, while those same people will rearrange breakfast and dinner plans so as not to miss the baseball practice, swimming lessons, and aerobic class?

The apostle is not teaching that we should neglect our family obligations, but he is making very clear that an eternal perspective will radically change when and how we spend our time together. While these relationships are as precious and meaningful as any earth affords, Jesus reminds us: "At the resurrection people will neither marry nor be given in marriage; they will be like the angels in heaven" (Matthew 22:30).

Calvin says:

> All the things which make for the enriching of this present life are sacred gifts of God, but we spoil them by our misuse of them. If we want to know the reason why, it is because we are always entertaining the delusion that we will go on forever in this world. The result is that the very things which ought to be of assistance to us in our pilgrimage through life, become the chains which bind us.[1]

So it is that the longing of Paul's heart is to see men and women given over to God's service without distraction, and the single life provides unique opportunities in this regard.

If you have never been married, he says, in 1 Corinthians 7, then singleness makes good sense. There are peculiar troubles that attach to marriage both in life and death; and while children sweeten our joys, they make our misfortunes more bitter (for example, in the death of our spouse). Paul is not suggesting that celibacy is a more spiritual road to go, but it may, in light of the context he describes, be more sensible. So there are practical advantages for those who have been given the gift of singleness, and one of these is that they do not have the distractions of family responsibilities. Now admittedly, they do not experience the benefits. But when the issue is a single focus on the work of the Lord, there can be no question that the freedom from distraction is a huge advantage.

I have an illustration of this even as I write. For the past week I have been on my own here on Lake Michigan. Removed from the delightful distractions of Sue and the children, I have been free to focus exclusively on this project without ever feeling that I was cheating either my wife or my children of the time. But the fact is, I am in one sense evading my responsibilities for a time for an agreed-upon objective. Were I single, I would not have any sense of obligation to which I must return. As a married man I have an inevitable two-fold concern: how to please my wife and care for her and how to please the Lord. The person who is single, free from this dual obligation, is therefore able to be more fully devoted to the Lord's work.

There is in all of this an implicit challenge to the single community to discover the vital role they can and should play in the purposes of God. It must surely be a strange sight from the portals of heaven to see singles preoccupied with roller-skating and dating and commiserating too often what they regard as their sorry lot in life. The single individual, whether that state continues through life or is interrupted by marriage, has a strategic opportunity to "seize the day" and serve the Lord unencumbered by the privileges and responsibilities that make up marriage.

THE ADVICE OF PARENTS AND OTHERS

You have probably discovered by now that few relationships you form will be neutral. In most cases, the person will have either a positive or a negative effect on you. Just think back to high school and you should recall examples of both types. This simple truth becomes more obvious as you continue to make friends—especially friends of the opposite gender. Perhaps by now you also realize the value of your parents' advice. (If you're like many people, parental guidance wasn't really sought out or heeded during the high school years.) But whether or not you agree with them, your parents speak from experience.

If your family structure has been molded by confusion and strife, consider finding other trusted adults within your wider family circle or church. People with unhappy home lives are particularly vulnerable to the temptation to hook up with someone prematurely as a means of escape. More often than not, these marriage partners have more negative than positive influence.

If you *do* choose to get married, your marriage will become an extremely high priority for you. It is likely to affect, and perhaps even negate, other things you had previously hoped to do. It's not that you won't do even better things, but just don't be naive enough to think marriage means you'll have a friend to "tag along" and do everything you always planned to do.

Wisdom comes from God (James 1:5). Don't leave a decision about whether or not to get married to instinct and logic. Be sure to see what God has to say about the matter. He may want to use you as a single person . . . or He may want to use you as a married person. Regardless of your marital state, you can be sure He wants to lead you through life and achieve all the potential with which He has gifted you.

AM I RUSHING INTO MARRIAGE?
AND, IF SO, WHY?

As an adviser to people wishing to be married, I am far more cautious during premarital counseling now than when I first began. I have witnessed an alarming number of broken marriages, and many of them failed in the early years. Consequently, a significant number of couples who go through our church's marriage preparation part company rather than get married. Our view is that we would rather see a split prior to marriage than to allow the couple to rush into marriage—and just as quickly into divorce. Essentially, we encourage couples to think through the same questions dealt with in this chapter. When they put serious thought into these matters, some of them cannot in good conscience commit to marriage.

One of the first danger signals as a couple approaches marriage is the "hurry-up offense." If two individuals have only known each other for a few months, more than likely their attraction is based on sheer emotion that may fade as quickly as it appeared. There are exceptions, of course, but in most cases they aren't ready to pledge themselves to each other for life. If their love for each other is genuine, they will be willing to wait and be sure. We ask couples to allow seven months of lead time in order to adequately complete the pre-marital process. Resistance to such advice is usually a danger sign.

Sadly, one of the reasons couples rush to get their marriage license is an unwillingness to establish and maintain sexual purity in the dating relationship. One of the tragic aspects of contemporary life is the number of young people who have become sexually sophisticated while remaining emotionally immature. Slowing down the process will often uncover these and other problem areas that must be dealt with if the marriage is going to have any chance of success.

ARE MY EXPECTATIONS REALISTIC?

"I know that once we are married, we'll be able to take care of that."

This statement, heard again and again, is usually fueled by wishful thinking rather than honest evaluation. If a young woman has never been able to balance her checkbook and has run up significant credit card debt, how realistic is it to expect that she can establish and maintain a frugal budget during marriage? If the young man's temper has frequently gotten him in trouble with teammates and authority figures, how can he assume that a marriage license will cure that? Or if the couple's dates have been almost all physical activity and little if any conversation, do they really think a wedding will "fix everything"?

It should come as no surprise that most people are on their best behavior during the dating phase. To be more honest, they aren't really themselves. They go out of their way to smile and accommodate—not wanting to risk offending the other person prematurely.

Potential life partners also need to see each other in various situations. Here are just a few:

- Late for an appointment because of congested traffic
- Visiting a hospitalized loved one
- Playing with the kids on the street
- Being around his or her parents
- Being around his or her "regular" friends
- Participating in a competitive sport
- Handling various stressful situations

It's not as if these things aren't going to come up during a marriage. The sooner one's prospective spouse sees how the other performs under such conditions, the better he or she can estimate the potential success of marriage. It's also good to have a few disagreements and arguments prior to the wedding. Otherwise, when they come up during marriage (and they will!) you will not be prepared to see the other person in this different light.

The more two people attempt to be real with each other, the more realistic their expectations will be as they enter marriage.

AM I MARRYING A PERSON OR A BODY?

This isn't exactly a frequently asked question, yet it is an important one for every potential bride or groom to consider. Western society is obsessed with externals: facial features, figure, muscular composition, weight, hairstyles, and so much more. Most magazines we pick up have an article related to our bodies. Consequently, young women quickly assume that their significance is directly related to their shape and dress size. Young men frequently model themselves after professional athletes and are disappointed with any features they feel rate less than "perfect." Essentially every model for products aimed at young people is tanned, attractive, and thin. The covert, yet clear, message is that how we look is more important than how we behave. Image is preferred over character and substance.

It therefore becomes very important for young people especially to determine whether the attraction they feel for their prospective spouse is *purely* physical. Now, clearly, no one would want to suggest that this aspect is irrelevant, but we must recognize that it does not deserve the attention it receives. So the more significant questions are:

- Do I enjoy conversing with this person?
- Can this person carry on an intelligent conversation?
- How do I feel when I introduce this person to some of my father's business associates?
- Is he or she a social misfit?
- Does this person have a growing interest in godly things, or is he or she still a spiritual infant?

These questions get to issues that are enduring. Age will take its toll on everyone. Physical beauty is passing. If we invest in a person who is little more than a physical "package," what will we do when that package begins to sag and droop over time?

The apostle Peter offered some good advice to the women of his day. He emphasized characteristics that are internal and mature with time:

> Your beauty should not come from outward adornment, such as braided hair and the wearing of gold jewelry and fine clothes. Instead, it should be that of

your inner self, the unfading beauty of a gentle and quiet spirit, which is of great worth in God's sight. For this is the way the holy women of the past who put their hope in God used to make themselves beautiful. (1 Peter 3:3–5)

In watching and listening to older couples, it quickly becomes apparent that their marriages endured the test of time because of an attraction based on depth of personality, not shallow physical appeal. They learned to share secrets as they treasured time spent together. They are happy to hang out together. There is no one they would rather have coffee with, for they have become best friends for life.

Physical intimacy and romantic love are not what keeps couples together. It's the emotional and spiritual aspects that make a marriage sweet.

WHAT SHOULD I LOOK FOR IN A HUSBAND?

This is no easy question to answer, yet it is an important one. While we could brainstorm any number of desired qualities, space only allows for some of the most essential traits. Here are the top six things women should look for in a potential husband.

1. **The man should be committed to growing in his relationship with Christ.**

Speaking for God, the prophet Amos asked: "Do two walk together unless they have agreed to do so?" (Amos 3:3). This question can be applied at many levels, not least of which is the lifelong commitment of marriage. It is difficult to overstate how vitally important this is.

Even secular research confirms the need for shared beliefs, attitudes, and values in order to have a successful marriage:

> According to David H. Olson, professor of family social science at the University of Minnesota, it's possible to predict as early as the day a couple becomes engaged whether that marriage will last. Olson questioned 164 courting couples on their values and checked again three years later. Fifty-two of them had never married, and of those who did, 31 had already separated, while 22 described their union as unhappy. After reviewing all of the initial interviews, Olson found he could identify which couples had been seriously mismatched. "People often believe that important differences will go away with time," says Olson, "but marriage does not automatically bring people closer."[2]

Some well-intentioned women enter marriage knowing the groom is not where he needs to be spiritually, but they intend to "take him on" as a discipleship project. Bad move. The intensity of a marriage relationship is challenging even for two spiritually mature people. It is far too great a challenge to learn to be a good husband and a good Christian simultaneously.

Women should not seek out husbands who merely have mastered "Bible trivia," but rather should look for those who are serious about growing in the grace and knowledge of the Lord Jesus (see 2 Peter 3:18). Does this mean that he should be more spiritually mature than she is? Ideally, yes. But if he isn't, prior to the marriage he should seek out a male mentor to help him prepare to fulfill the God-given role of husband and spiritual leader.

2. A husband should be an individual of obvious integrity.

Many years ago I was staying with a family when a young man came for a date with one of the daughters. While waiting for her, he sat confidently in the living room and talked with the mother. He boasted about how well he was doing in sales and explained how it was necessary to tell "little white lies" to customers. For example, to keep from losing business to the competition, he would promise delivery dates when he knew there was no possibility of meeting them. He seemed quite pleased with himself.

The girl was drawn to his good looks and eager for a relationship. They went out on the date, and eventually the two of them got married. Sadly, their decision was premature, and a messy divorce followed. The girl had known about the guy's predilection for little untruths, but wasn't concerned. In the interest of advancing the relationship, she figured she could get married first and work on her husband later. But she discovered that he was much more masterful at deceit than she had expected. The marriage crumbled around them.

No matter how some men try to justify their use of untruths, those lies should serve as neon signs to prospective brides. What makes us think that if a person would lie to a customer, a boss, a teacher, or a parent, he wouldn't also lie to a wife? Women should watch and listen closely when they enter a serious dating relationship. It should be patently obvious that a prospective husband is honest to the core. If he isn't, the woman should keep looking until she finds one who is.

3. A husband should be able to lead boldly.

Not everyone will be able to marry the high school quarterback or the class president. That's not the kind of leadership to which I'm referring. Every woman should look for the kind of man who can think for himself, weigh options, and make good decisions.

Clearly, no one person *always* makes the best decisions. We all make mistakes. Many times good leadership requires willingness to take counsel, change one's mind, and then proceed with a different course of action. So don't expect perfection in a husband.

Nor should a woman settle for "leadership" that is selfish and domineering. Christian leadership is marked by an attitude of servanthood and submission to others. On the other hand, a young woman should be more than a little concerned if the man she is dating has to check with his mother constantly before deciding where to eat or which T-shirt to buy!

A woman should witness genuine affection between the man and his family members, but at the same time she should detect a readiness on his part to step out on his own. It is unlikely that he will ever cleave to his wife if he is unable to leave his family.

4. A husband should display the ability to love sacrificially.

Women should seek out men who display the quality of self-sacrifice without feeling the need to say, "I'm a very self-sacrificing person, you know!" Self-sacrifice is detected in subtle ways that vary from person to person.

Watch at the end of an evening with friends to see if he is quick to organize and spearhead the cleanup. Listen carefully as his elderly aunt mentions whether her nephew has been faithful in his visits to the nursing home. Observe the way he relates to children, his willingness to hold doors for passersby with full arms, and his attitude with waitresses and other service people. Watch his eyes as he sits in a café and observes the obvious ravages of AIDS in the body of the young man at the counter.

Most prospective husbands will express the intent to sacrifice for their wives. However, if a woman detects that a man hasn't practiced this attitude with other people, she has the right to be wary.

5. A husband should be able to laugh heartily.

Humor is a vital element in preventing marital failure. The ability to laugh does not mean being a class clown or even a joke teller. In fact, the poor guy may be hopeless at telling jokes, needing the woman's help when he forgets punch lines and gets vacant stares. But it *is* important that he like to laugh.

A key trait to look for is his willingness to laugh at himself. If he takes himself too seriously, a marriage will probably have problems. Can he tell a story where someone else is obviously the hero while he comes off looking foolish? Is he willing to reveal pictures of himself when his teeth protruded and his ears stuck out—in much the same way they still do? And when he laughs at the comic misfortunes of others, can he do so without becoming cruel or crude?

In *Ragman: And Other Cries of Faith,*[3] Walter Wangerin tells of how he and his wife lived in a small apartment when they were first married. Whenever they had a disagreement he would storm out and walk around the block until he cooled down.

One time he trapped his coat as he slammed the door behind him. It was raining, so he had two options. He could slip the coat off and walk in the rain without it, or he could ring the bell and have his wife open the door. Choosing the latter course of action, he rang the bell. As the door opened his wife was laughing uncontrollably, realizing what had happened. In that moment, he writes, he could simply have laughed with her and humor would have provided the bridge to reconciliation. But refusing to do so, he gathered up his coat and walked off into the rainy evening, a prisoner to his own refusal to laugh.

We all face opportunities to make those decisions whether or not to laugh at ourselves. We don't always get it right the first time, but we can learn to do so with a little practice. A husband who cannot laugh when *he* makes a mistake is not likely to be any less severe with his wife's blunders.

6. A husband should model genuine humility.

Oscar Wilde was asked by the customs officer at an airport whether he had anything to declare. His reply was, "Nothing except my genius!" How would you like to live with someone who had that kind of attitude?

Simply put, a good husband should not be stuck on himself, and his attitude should be genuine. Watch out for people who attempt to manufacture humility by debasing themselves. Such people constantly declare their shortcomings and inabilities in order to draw attention to themselves. Even when the focus in on "my" big mistakes, "my" failures, and "my" lack of talent, the emphasis remains on "me." Those people hope to have others contradict their negative statements and make a big fuss over them.

Genuine humility keeps its focus on other people. Watch to see if the other person can share the joy of a competitor's success. Can he be a good understudy without being critical of the person to whom he reports. Does he discuss the talents of his co-workers, or only their faults? Does he enjoy the competition of sports, or does he make excuses every time he loses?

Humility can also be detected in his prayer life and in the way he approaches opportunities for which he is naturally talented. Is it clear that he really believes that the fear of the Lord is the beginning of wisdom? Does he really believe that apart from the Lord's enabling he can do nothing?

The absence of humility can be quickly detected. So can the presence of false humility.

This list of what to look for in a husband is clearly selective and by no means exhaustive. But these factors make an excellent beginning to a checklist.

WHAT SHOULD I LOOK FOR IN A WIFE?

Again, any list I provide for such a broad question is going to be selective, but I believe the following aspects are six of the most important things men should look for in a potential wife.

1. A good wife must have personal faith and trust in the Lord Jesus.

I begin this list with the same requirement as the list for prospective husbands. It is the basis for any and all other qualities on the list.

It is hard to overstate the importance of ensuring that we not enter into an intimate relationship where one person is a Christian and the other is not. The Bible refers to this situation as being "unequally yoked" (2 Corinthians 6:14, KJV). Jay Adams explains:

> To be unequally yoked is to be unable to pull together. That means two divergent standards, two opposite goals, two radically different interpretations of life, two incompatible masters to serve, and two contrary powers at work. Unbelief allied with belief in Christ means just one thing—there can be no real intimacy in matters that really count. The two cannot pull together because they are not truly together.[4]

Paul commands believers to marry "only in the Lord" (1 Corinthians 7:39, KJV). A marriage with only half the people committed to godly things cannot be regarded as "in the Lord." Young men wanting a wife need the same warning as women looking for a husband. It's not as common as the reverse situation, yet sometimes a man finds himself in a deepening friendship with an unbelieving woman. Despite the counsel he receives to the contrary, he desperately wants to believe that he will win her over to Christianity once they become husband and wife. More often than not, the woman makes little effort to pursue spiritual things once the rings are on her finger. The man is left to go to church and work on his spiritual life alone —or worse yet, to eventually stop trying altogether.

2. A wife should possess beauty that is deeper than the skin.

I don't know of anyone who sets out to find a spouse who is physically unattractive, yet it is important to remember that beauty is often in the eye of the beholder.

Earlier in this chapter, I quoted from Peter's letter about the importance of "a gentle and quiet spirit." A wise man looks for a woman who possesses a natural radiance rather than a glow which comes from a bottle. It is less important to find a woman whose beauty comes from time spent in front of a beauty parlor mirror than someone who is regularly before the mirror of the Word of God.

I recall walking on the beach with Sue's dad before she and I were even engaged. Sue was out in the water. As we reached the spot where she was swimming, she walked toward us, tossed her head back, and shook the water from her long hair. Her father said, "What a beautiful girl inside and outside!" I agreed with his opinion then, and I still do!

While external features might get our attention, it's the person's inner qualities that should cause the real attraction.

3. A wife should be an initiative taker with an attitude of submission.

This parallels the previous statement that the man should be a sacrificial leader. A wise man desires a woman with ideas, abilities, hopes, plans, and dreams—a whole panorama of abilities she brings to marriage. In many areas he will be dependent upon her knowledge, insight, courage, faith, and expertise.

The word *submission* is so frequently misunderstood that it has become a sensitive issue for many people. God's intended role for the wife, as I discuss in a later chapter, is not to wait around for her husband's directives, as if somehow she were paralyzed without them. She is God's gift to the man as a companion and helper. There will seldom be a day when he does not have occasion to thank God for his wife's wisdom and grace.

However, it is also important not to fall into the clutches of a bossy, self-opinionated woman who is clearly unprepared to submit her heart, mind, and lifestyle to the clear teaching of God's Word. Some of the radical elements of feminism have been accepted by certain sectors of the church, even though they are in conflict with God's Word. Later in this book we will see how the roles of husband and wife are not interchangeable. Certain expectations for each role are clearly spelled out.

4. A wife's behavior should build her husband's confidence.

Trustworthiness stems from character. A woman's intrinsic qualities are revealed by her actions. She knows, for example, the difference between dressing to look attractive and deliberately trying to appear seductive. When a man tells me his wife chooses swimsuits that make her the object of male attention at the neighborhood pool, I know there are serious issues that need to be faced in that marriage.

A woman concerned with purity and reverence will always be alluring to a godly man. Even if she becomes a Christian after marriage, such qualities will be instrumental in convincing her husband to become a believer as well.

One key to trustworthy behavior is a controlled tongue. Some women are known for their capacity to gossip and slander. A man who wants to get married will do well to look for a woman whose speech is full of wisdom. It is much easier to put one's complete trust and confidence in such a person.

5. A wife should display kindness that touches others.

While women do not have exclusive ownership of the characteristic of kindness, it seems that they do a much better job of expressing compassion than most men do. It appears that God has fashioned women to be capable of special tenderness. Men are frequently intent to "keep moving" and get to where they are going. Women are usually more willing to stop in the cause of compassion.

No doubt we can list a number of women in our lives who have at one time or another impressed us with their tenderness. It might be harder to form such a long list of men. When Paul wanted to emphasize the extent of the gentleness he and his fellow ministers had tried to show one group of people, he compared it to the gentleness of a mother caring for her little children (1 Thessalonians 2:7).

As our culture continues to promote effeminate men and masculine women, we as Christians must be prepared in the face of ridicule, abuse, and probably persecution, to be unashamed in holding firm to the guidelines of Scripture when it comes to these things. There were very clear reasons for the Old Testament commands relating to the distinction between the sexes, and we do well to pay more careful attention to them at this time.

6. A wife should have a sense of humor that braves adversity.

This is another area that is equally important for men and women. The ability to laugh will get the couple through more than a few rough spots.

One of the qualities of "the wife of noble character" described in Proverbs 31 is that "she is clothed with strength and dignity; she can laugh at the days to come" (v. 25). Along with this ability, the passage explains that she is tender, but also tough. She can oversee numerous projects and handle all the variables. When the threat of discouragement or destruction looms, she is able to chuckle to herself because her dependence is upon God. She doesn't rely on her charm. She recognizes that physical beauty is fleeting, but that fact doesn't cause her to curl up in a ball or slump on a psychologist's couch. No, she laughs at the days to come.

It's no different now than it was in the days of Solomon. How blessed is the man who finds such a woman!

WHERE AM I SUPPOSED TO FIND A MATE LIKE THIS?

If you wanted to meet tennis players, you would probably try a tennis club. So in seeking to meet Christians who live out the qualities previously described, the best place will be church. While seeking a mate for life is not in itself a sufficient reason for attending church, it is still a legitimate motivation in staying for coffee or joining a singles' group. Do not kid yourself that you are above such an approach.

I advise people to allow others to help them in their search for the right husband or wife. While we should never marry someone in order to please a third party, we should at least be willing to listen to the insights of those who know us best. As Sue and I watch our children grow, it is not difficult to determine which of their companions would be most likely to benefit them in marriage.

Siblings can also watch out for each other when it comes to potential life mates. My mother died when my sisters were fifteen and eleven. As an older brother, I took a peculiar interest in who they dated. Now, through the providence of God, I can say that Sue and I had a part in introducing both of them to the Christian men they married.

And finally, mature couples can play a role in helping their single friends. Some couples attempt to become matchmakers, but they can do much more by opening their homes to allow singles to meet one another in a nonthreatening environment. Also, the single people are offered a bird's-eye view of what marriage can be as they see it modeled in their hosts.

WHAT AM I SUPPOSED
TO DO ABOUT MY SEXUAL FEELINGS?

The Bible is perfectly clear that sex is intended only within the context of marriage. In dating, it is important not to anticipate marriage in this sexual dimension. Do not be double-minded about this. How can you expect to marry a virgin if every other fellow you know is showing such scant regard for a girl's purity as you are doing in dating? You do not have to be sexually pure for the next five years, just for the next five minutes! To isolate sexual intercourse from the emotional, spiritual, psychological, and volitional elements of marriage is to create a monstrosity. Have a close friend hold you accountable. Deal with your feelings at an early point before they sweep you past the boundaries you have set for yourself.

Perhaps you've already crossed those boundaries—if not into promiscuous sexual activity, at least into areas where you are not comfortable. If so, there needs to be repentance and restoration and the establishing of holy habits.

One reason sexual sin is so hard to overcome is that it often emerges from a habitually impure thought life. If our thoughts are continually on sexual involvement with others, it's difficult to act otherwise. Unless we deal ruthlessly and immediately with the problem, the chances for repeat behavior are high.

Sinful patterns of behavior are very resistant to discovery and correction because habitual activity tends to take place unconsciously, frequently, and automatically. Where there has been genuine repentance, then we need to follow Paul's example: "Forgetting what is behind and straining toward what is ahead, I press on toward the goal to win the prize for which God has called me heavenward in Christ Jesus" (Philippians 3:13–14).

Sexual drives can be strong. God is far, far stronger.

WHAT IF I'M NOT ROMANTICALLY ATTRACTED TO ANOTHER PERSON?

What are we to say to the single person who sees all his or her friends falling in love and getting married, yet never personally feels a romantic attraction toward anyone? I'll leave this answer to writer and theologian John Stott, who is himself single:

> What about us? We too must accept this teaching, however hard it may seem, as God's purpose both for us and for society. We shall not become a bundle of frustrations and inhibitions if we embrace God's standard but only if we rebel against it. Christ's yoke is easy, provided we submit to it. It is possible for human sexual energy to be redirected both into affectionate relationships with friends of both sexes and into the loving service of others. Alongside a natural loneliness accompanied sometimes by acute pain, we can find joyful self-fulfillment in the self-giving service of God and other people.[5]

Don't worry if you don't feel the same romantic leanings as most of your other friends. God creates all kinds of people for all kinds of purposes. You can do far more harm trying to force yourself to be like "everyone else" than if you determine to fulfill God's plan for you as a unique individual.

CHAPTER THREE

SEALED
WITH A VOW

When I meet a couple to finalize the details of their wedding ceremony, one question always arises: Will they use the traditional vows or substitute something of their own creation? When they decide on the latter course, the challenge is then to ensure that what they say will not only express how they are feeling, but will also convey the commitment of their wills.

Many people never realize that during the wedding ceremony they are never asked how they *feel* about the person they are marrying. Sometimes it is necessary to wean a young woman away from a heartfelt emotional speech she has been working on for months in preparation for her big day. But no matter how eloquent and flowery the speech, it's not a vow unless it involves a willful commitment to the other person.

When the Bible speaks of love within marriage, it is always presented as a result of the person's will, not a "here-today, gone-tomorrow" emotion. Nowhere in the Bible do we discover romantic love as the foundation for marriage. The biblical model is much more akin to the "arranged marriage" system we hear about in other cultures. In such cases, the family members determine who is best suited for their son, daughter, brother, or sister. The "betrothed" person is then expected to make the marriage work. In stark contrast is our Western arrangement where newly engaged individuals stun their friends and family by announcing the name of a person with whom they are planning on spending the rest of their lives!

It's not that either system is automatically better than the other. But when marriages are founded on emotional surges and physical attractions, they are wide open to the possibility of disintegration when warm feelings evaporate and bodies succumb to the ravaging effects of gravity! On the other hand, the likelihood of survival is markedly improved when marriages are grounded in friendship, companionship, and the awareness of an unending covenant, no matter what.

Therefore, the vows become very important. They provide walls of protection when threatening emotional winds and waves begin to beat upon the relationship. The traditional vows have stood the test of time because they aptly summarize the commitment that is involved.

Husband and wife have a duty to one another to abide by the vows they made in the presence of God and before their family and friends. A faithfulness to the vows is automatically a faithfulness to each other.

The lyrics of Beth Nielsen Chapman's song "Faithful Heart" emphasize the importance of wedding vows in connection to faithfulness:

Faithful heart, what more can one life ask
One hand to hold along life's path
Share with me this vow
And for all time
Our souls will be entwined

I give this love, I live this love
No greater joy is mine
Storms will come, but we will never part
For each of us bequeath a faithful heart

Before having potential marriage partners repeat the vows, the minister inquires about their intentions. He essentially asks them if they want to be married. Since they are only minutes away from the "I do's," one always hopes for an affirmative answer. But these questions of intent are not to be taken lightly. The couple needs to ponder them carefully prior to the ceremony in prospect of saying yes to the obligations of marriage.

Many marriage failures would be avoided if couples understood just what they were getting into. The expectations need to be clarified early on so there is plenty of preparation time to work through the implications of such radical, life-changing commitments.

Let's take a close-up look at the traditional wedding vows. In most cases, the man and woman are asked the same basic questions with one notable exception on the woman's part.

WILL YOU HAVE THIS PERSON TO BE YOUR LAWFUL WEDDED WIFE/HUSBAND?

This first question distinguishes clearly between cohabitation (what used to be referred to as "living in sin") and the legal status of marriage. The transaction, made under God and in keeping with the laws of the state, alters irrevocably one's single state. Marriage brings about a definite and significant change for both individuals.

It also becomes clear that any previous pre-marital sexual encounters are not to be equated with marriage. Sex outside of marriage secures one of the benefits of marriage in isolation from all the obligation that God intends. God's plan is one of "leaving and cleaving." Marriage is not simply legalized lust. Because of its divine origin, it is not to be entered upon lightly or carelessly. One seldom sees on church notice boards the once familiar phraseology: Marriages Solemnized.

In order to further reinforce the legal nature of what is taking place, the minister is charged with the responsibility of inquiring if either the couple or the congregation knows of any just reason why they may not be *lawfully* joined in marriage. Marriage is not just a sacred rite. It is a legal action as well.

WILL YOU LIVE TOGETHER AFTER GOD'S ORDINANCE IN THE HOLY ESTATE OF MARRIAGE?

Marriage is to take place between a man and a woman. The Bible clearly condemns any notion of homosexuality. The idea of monogamous same-sex relationships being acceptable to God emerges from an unwillingness to submit to the clear teaching of Scripture. We are not at liberty to redefine marriage on the basis of the changing mores of contemporary culture.

The importance of this portion of the wedding vow immediately becomes apparent when one thinks ahead and imagines circumstances that will sorely try a commitment to companionship and intimacy. Solomon warns his son about "the wayward wife with her seductive words, who has left the partner of her youth and ignored the covenant she made before God" (Proverbs 2:16–17). It is for this reason that we cannot constantly be redefining marriage in order to suit the mood of the moment.

A human contract may be terminated at any time for a variety of reasons. If marriage is approached with this same attitude, it hardly has a chance. Only the settled conviction that one's obligation to a spouse is based on God's ordinance will provide the necessary framework to work through difficulties without calling it quits.

WILL YOU LOVE, HONOR, AND KEEP THE OTHER PERSON?

Once again, a biblical understanding of *love* is vital. If we accept the viewpoint of one secular song, that love is simply "a secondhand emotion," then we will constantly be in danger of throwing in the towel. But when love becomes a series of actions that fulfill our vows, we rise above the tyranny of emotional ups and downs.

On their wedding day, it is hard for a couple to believe that the issue of love is even included in the question. They are about to explode with all kinds of manifestations of their love. It is virtually impossible for them to grasp the notion of a deeper dimension of love that will be needed as months give way to years and sheer emotion is replaced by willful commitment.

And what of the matter of *honoring* one another? Can a husband fulfill this requirement by simply being a good financial provider while serving his own selfish interests in the pursuit of hobbies? Can five days a year with his wife in New England compensate for the fact that he spent his last twenty wedding anniversaries fishing with his father and his brother? Absolutely not!

The husband honors his wife by putting her first, considering her interests before his own, and finding his greatest joy in seeing her blossom within marriage to the fullness of all that God intends. The wife honors her spouse by becoming "husband-oriented" in all she does.[1]

When a man and woman honor one another in these ways, it saves them from the contemporary idea of "being one's own person." Reciprocating honor allows them to discover the wonderful ability to become truly united.

The commitment to *keep* the other person is another expression of covenant companionship. A hedge of protection is established by a husband and wife as they watch out for each other's best interests, saving the other person from foolish choices, and taking responsibility for the other's well-being. This type of friendship and cooperation is well expressed in the words of the preacher:

> Two are better than one,
> because they have a good return for their work:
> If one falls down,
> his friend can help him up.
> But pity the man who falls and has no one to help him up!
> Also, if two lie down together, they will keep warm.
> But how can one keep warm alone?
> Though one may be overpowered,
> two can defend themselves.
> A cord of three strands is not quickly broken.
>
> (Ecclesiastes 4:9–12)

IN SICKNESS AND IN HEALTH

The apostle Paul reminds us of the natural process of decay: "Outwardly we are wasting away"

(2 Corinthians 4:16). The wear and tear on our bodies will confront us all, particularly in old age. It's a simple fact of life, but it may become a severe test of marriage. I like what Erma Bombeck had to say on this issue:

> Illness has to be one of the tests of a marriage. That's why they put it in the marriage vows. Everyone sort of glides over it, but it's important. For the first time you are caught naked with your pretenses down. You are vulnerable and you are dependent. Neither of you married to have the other partner "take care of you." You were supposed to be a team. And now you are being seen in a compromising scene with your head hung into a toilet bowl at 2 A.M. while another person stands over you, taking away any shred of modesty or mystique you have left.[2]

In addition to such "normal" expectations of sickness, some marriage partners face especially intense strains when the other person's illness challenges emotional and financial limits. The effects can be devastating. This is especially true when such severe illness strikes early in the person's marriage rather than late in life. Hopes are high, dreams are fresh, and children are rich with potential. Yet the joy that was anticipated is replaced by a sore trial.

I have a friend who just lost his young wife to

brain cancer, following a prolonged illness. In caring for her and his young children, he has been a striking model of faithfulness to his marriage vows through God's enabling power. Another of my friends from college has been in a wheelchair and dependent on the loving faithfulness of his wife for more than ten years.

Thousands of husbands and wives live with the peculiar challenge of their partners' blindness, multiple sclerosis, depression, and other numerous illnesses. Many bear living testimony to their commitment to the covenant companionship of their wedding vows. How different they are from those who seek out the services of Dr. Kevorkian as they face similar illnesses, but usually without any kind of support from their spouses.

Recently one of my colleagues shared with me the remarkable response of Robertson McQuilken to the illness of his wife:

> Seventeen summers ago, Muriel and I began our journey into the twilight. It's midnight now, at least for her, and sometimes I wonder when dawn will break. Even the dread Alzheimer's disease isn't supposed to attack so early and torment so long. Yet, in her silent world, Muriel is so content, so lovable. If Jesus took her home, how I would miss her gentle, sweet presence. Yes, there are times when I get irritated, but not often. It doesn't make sense to get angry.

And besides, perhaps the Lord has been answering the prayer of my youth to mellow my spirit.

Once, though, I completely lost it. In the days when Muriel could still stand and walk and we had not resorted to diapers, sometimes there were "accidents." I was on my knees beside her, trying to clean up the mess as she stood, confused, by the toilet. It would have been easier if she weren't so insistent on helping. I got more and more frustrated. Suddenly, to make her stand still, I slapped her calf—as if that would do any good. It wasn't a hard slap, but she was startled. I was, too. Never in our 44 years of marriage had I ever so much as touched her in anger or in rebuke of any kind. Never; wasn't even tempted, in fact. But now, when she needed me most . . .

Sobbing, I pled with her to forgive me—no matter that she didn't understand words any better than she could speak them. So I turned to the Lord to tell Him how sorry I was. It took me days to get over it. Maybe God bottled those tears to quench the fires that might ignite again some day.

It wasn't long before I found myself in the same condition, on the floor in the bathroom. Muriel wanted to help—hadn't cleaning up messes been her specialty? But now those busy hands didn't know exactly what to do. I mopped frantically, trying to fend off the interfering hands, and contemplated how best to get a soiled slip over a head that was totally opposed to the idea. At that moment Chuck Swindoll boomed from the radio in the kitchen, "Men! Are you at home? *Really* at home?" In the midst of my stinking immersion I smiled, "Yeah, Chuck, I really am." Do I ever wish I weren't?

Recently, a student wife asked me, "Don't you ever get tired?"

"Tired? Every night. That's why I go to bed."

"No, I mean tired of . . ." and she tilted her head toward Muriel, who sat silently in her wheelchair, her vacant eyes saying, "No one at home just now." I responded to the question, "Why, no, I don't get tired. I love to care for her. She's my precious."

"Well, I certainly would."

Cindi and her husband are handsome, healthy, smart people, and yet she admits that it is hard constantly to affirm one another. What happens when there is so little to commend? How does love make a difference?

Love is said to evaporate if the relationship is not mutual, if it's not physical, if the other person doesn't communicate, or if one party doesn't carry his or her share of the load. When I hear the litany of essentials for a happy marriage, I count off what my beloved can no longer contribute, and I contemplate how truly mysterious love is. . . .

Valentine's Day was always special at our house because that was the day in 1948 Muriel accepted my marriage proposal. On the eve of Valentine's Day in 1995 I read a statement by some specialist that Alzheimer's is the most cruel disease of all, but that the victim is actually the caregiver. I wondered why I never felt like a victim. That night I entered in my journal: "The reason I don't feel like a victim is—I'm not!" When others urged me to call it quits, I responded, "Do you realize how lonely I would be without her?"

After I bathed Muriel on her bed that Valentine's eve and kissed her good night (she still enjoys two things: good food and kissing!), I whispered a prayer over her: "Dear Jesus, you love sweet Muriel more than I, so please keep my beloved through the night; may she hear the angel choirs."

The next morning I was peddling on my Exercycle at the foot of her bed and reminiscing about some of our happy lovers' days long gone while Muriel slowly emerged from sleep. Finally, she popped awake and, as she often does, smiled at me. Then, for the first time in months she spoke, calling out to me in a voice clear as a crystal chime, "Love . . . love . . . love." I jumped from my cycle and ran to embrace her. "Honey, you really do love me, don't you?" Holding me with her eyes and patting my back, she responded with the only words she could find to respond positively: "I'm nice," she said.

Those may prove to be the last words she ever spoke.[3]

AND FORSAKING ALL OTHERS, KEEP YOURSELF ONLY UNTO HIM/HER

An affirmative response to this statement indicates a commitment to a lifelong relationship with one person. It acknowledges that the God-given context for sexual intercourse is that of a heterosexual, monogamous marriage.

Monogamy may not sound like much fun, certainly not in comparison to its alternative. *Monogamy.* Sounds an awful lot like *monotony,* doesn't it? Or *monopoly?* Do I hear *mahogany?* Yet we dare not relate monogamy to tedium, an endless board game, or a great aunt's dining table. True happiness—the deep, sustaining contentment we seek—lies somewhere down "Monogamy Road."[4]

In order to say yes to absolute faithfulness, we must say no to a number of other options. We say no to *fornication,* which is sex prior to marriage. We say no to *adultery,* which is sex outside of marriage. And we say no to *homosexuality,* which is beyond marriage. Such a stance immediately sets us apart from the standards and preoccupations of our surrounding culture.

The Bridges of Madison County was a bestselling book and a major film. Yet the plot is nothing more than a sorry tale of adultery disguised in the wrappings of romance.

The Old Testament made clear the sanctity of marriage: "You shall not commit adultery" (Exodus 20:14). The commandment is not a prohibition aimed at holding down man's evil sexual lusts, but a positive protection for full troth fulfillment. (*Troth* is an old-fashioned word conveying the notion of undying loyalty or unwavering commitment.) The seventh commandment affirms that only in troth and fidelity can marriage be a blessing. Today it should perhaps read: "Keep the troth in marriage," or even, "Have fun in marriage."

Marriage does not shatter as easily as crystal glass, so some people flirt with the idea that fidelity is not really affected by an indiscretion here and there. But adultery always breaks troth, destroys mutual freedom, and makes people unhappy. Scripture warns against it to protect marriage. The commandment is much like a No Swimming sign planted in front of a dangerous pond. The signs go up because someone cares enough about life to try to prevent tragedy.

As God forbids adultery, He calls marriage partners to more than physical fidelity. "Marriage is a total troth communion that can be broken by various kinds of infidelity, not just physical [indiscretions], as we have traditionally too often assumed."[5] When Paul wrote to the Thessalonian believers, he put things very plainly: "It is God's will that you should be sanctified: that you should avoid sexual immorality" (1 Thessalonians 4:3).

He was writing from Corinth, which was infamous for its immorality. The temple to Aphrodite, the Greek goddess of sex and beauty, dominated the skyline of the city. Shrine prostitutes plied their trade on the streets of Corinth under cover of darkness. Thessalonica had its own pagan deities called Cabiri, which were honored through rites of gross immorality. Men were not expected to limit their sexual participation to only their wives. Yet then, as now, Scripture provided plain, honest, practical, authoritative, and uninhibited instruction on the matter of marital faithfulness for God's people.

Statistics tell us that more than half of our nation's men and a third of the women engage in extramarital affairs.[6] Although Christians plead for traditional values with purity before and fidelity after marriage, it appears that we are losing ground to the myths and lies of our generation, and parents are disappointing and devastating their children at an alarming rate. The media is filled with nonsense on this topic. For example, here is an article I filed *twenty years ago.* It is by Jill Tweedie, a columnist for the *Guardian* newspaper in England. It began like this:

> The divorce rate goes up every year and up rise the pundits too, blaming our godlessness, our selfishness, our lustfulness. They threaten us with the imminent breakdown of family life and the end of society as we know it. But I don't accept what they say. In my view, the divorce rate is going up for one obvious reason: The kind of marriage we are expected to support simply doesn't suit us any more; it falls apart because it has become a sort of anti-life structure, a cage. I don't

doubt that most human beings want and thrive on a loving sexual relationship between individuals, one man and one woman. Where I differ drastically with the pundits is in expecting that relationship to last as long as they both shall live, and labeling as failures those who commit the crime of loving and then loving again. I think this expectation goes against our deepest nature, stunting our growth and making demands upon us that require distorted lives to fulfill.[7]

Tweedie expresses herself very clearly, giving voice to an opinion that has becoming increasingly popular in the ensuing years. The Maker's instructions as set out in Scripture are summarily dismissed, and the God-intended structure for the basis of human society is disregarded as a cage—a sort of "anti-life structure"! Tweedie's article concluded with her dreams for the future: "Outside the bonds of Christian marriage we will, I hope, learn for the first time what love is all about."[8]

Even earlier, in 1969, sociologist Morton Hunt suggested that polygamy was better suited to the emotional capacities and requirements of many people, particularly men. He wrote: "It offers renewal, excitement, and continuance of expressions of personal rediscovery; it is an answer to the boredom of lifelong monogamy. We are by nature polygamous."[9]

The confusion of our culture has sadly infiltrated too many of our homes and churches, attempting to cloud the absolute clarity of the Bible. Marriage is not a sacrament; it is a creation ordinance. In other words, it was given to all of humanity at creation, and not only to Christians. It is God's design for the continuance of the human race. Its status as an institution is conferred by God, and its standard is set by Him. Marriage, we learn, is supposed to be a model of Christ's love for the church. It is to be based not upon lust, but upon honor and holiness (Ephesians 5).

We should never doubt the sanctity of marriage. As we have seen, the Bible makes clear that marriage is not simply a convenient, contractual relationship which two people may terminate at will. Rather, they are joined together by God and become one flesh. The level of intimacy should be like two persons becoming one person. It is therefore a tragic violation of this union when one of the parties engages in an extramarital affair. In committing adultery, the person sins against God, his or her own body, the partner in the affair, a spouse, and the partner's spouse. It is not the prerogative of either party to treat marriage like old clothes and discard it at the first signs of wear and tear, starting over with someone else.

We should also be on guard against the fuzzy thinking that concludes that there is no difference between *thoughts* of adultery and actual *physical* involvement with someone other than our marriage partner. We certainly cannot argue with Jesus' statement in His Sermon on the Mount: "I tell you that anyone who looks at a woman lustfully has already committed adultery with her in his heart" (Matthew 5:28). Yet some people willfully misinterpret this verse: "I've thought about having an affair, so I'm guilty of it. I guess I may as well go ahead and do it."

We have to realize that there are vast differences between the *thought* of adultery and the *act* of adultery. Literal adultery breaks the marriage covenant; adulterous thoughts do not. Adultery provides grounds for divorce; mental adultery does not. Adultery violates and defiles two people's bodies; its mental counterpart does not. Adultery is a vehicle for the transmission of disease; thinking about it is not.

Of course, if we're having continual thoughts of committing adultery with someone, that's a symptom that something isn't right in our lives or our marriages. That's why it is so imperative that we heed Jesus' warning to rid ourselves of such destructive thoughts which may lead to the actuality of the sinful event. The longer we allow fantasies to float through our minds without dealing with them, the more likely we are to yield when actual temptation presents itself.

In the case studies that opened chapter 1, there was little if any indication at first that those casual friendships were headed for disaster. The main problem was that the married party in each case failed to cling rigorously to the commitment previously made to his or her spouse. Each relationship started out innocently enough, but the people involved gradually began to depend on each other emotionally. They began to share private plans and hopes. They justified lunches together and exchanged physical touches that were, they assured themselves, "like brother and sister." They liked each other, became special to each other, and eventually were unwilling to control the juggernaut of their emotional and physical drives.

In order to be successful in happily maintaining the monogamous aspect of marital faithfulness, a number of factors are crucial:

- We need to remind ourselves that we live in God's presence (Psalm 139). Wasn't this part of the secret of Joseph's success? When he faced fierce temptation, he exclaimed: "How then could I do such a wicked thing and sin against God?" (Genesis 39:9).

- We need to feed on a steady diet of the Word of God. "How can a young man keep his way pure? By living according to your word" (Psalm 119:9).

- We need to be regularly in the company of the people of God. Hebrews 10:25 reminds us: "Let us not give up meeting together, . . . but let us encourage one another." Isolation tends to create opportunities for temptation and potential sexual indiscretion. Involvement with other Christians is an ideal antidote. While the danger is not completely removed, there is less likelihood for failure in this area when we are meaningfully involved in the lives of others.

- We should never allow the lifestyle and thought patterns of ungodly neighbors and work associates to capture our minds. Paul put it succinctly: "Do not be misled: 'Bad company corrupts good character'" (1 Corinthians 15:33).

SO LONG AS YOU BOTH SHALL LIVE

Marriage is a life and death issue. It is a life-long commitment that is only to be ended by death. Despite the clarity of this concluding statement of the wedding vow, an alarming number of couples apparently determine that this part is optional. Instead of facing difficulties and setbacks with a "for life" mentality, they are immediately on the lookout for loopholes and escape clauses.

Anyone who plays golf soon discovers the "out of bounds" rule. White stakes on each side of the fairway provide clear demarcation between what is in play and what is not. However, there are a few contingencies (such as ground under repair and certain hazards) that provide for a "free drop" after a ball has gone out of bounds. Similarly, the Bible generally rules divorce "out of bounds," yet makes allowances for it under certain specific conditions. However, the prevailing emphasis of Scripture is on staying the course and seeing a marriage through to the end.

The topic of divorce caused heated debate even in Jesus' day. The Pharisees could not agree among themselves, and they came to test Jesus about the issue (Matthew 19:1–12). One school of thought was very liberal and allowed divorce for anything that displeased the husband. If his wife burned the meal, used too much salt in preparation, or went in the street without her veil, the husband could divorce her freely. The other school of thought was much more conservative. On the basis of Deuteronomy 24, these scholars argued that unchastity was the only legitimate reason for divorce.

In replying, Jesus first pointed out that the underlying emphasis of their question was wrong. He addressed the question of divorce by looking at the broader issue of marriage. He reminded them that by creation ordinance, God has declared marriage an indissoluble union. It is a divine institution, not to be tampered with.

Marriage is not a contract of temporary convenience that can be dissolved at will. Divorce breaks a seal that has been engraved by the hand of God. The commitment to marriage by a man and a woman is for life, underwritten by God and not to be tampered with by humans. The bottom line is: *Do not get divorced.* Do not entertain it as a possibility. When marriage partners find themselves in difficulty, it is imperative that they commit themselves to the marriage in the firm belief that God is able to rekindle, restore, and renew.

But the liberal Pharisees weren't satisfied with Jesus' answer. They asked, "What about when Moses commanded that a man give his wife a certificate of divorce?" (see v. 7). Like so many people today they were far more interested in the loophole than in maintaining a focus on the sanctity of the marriage bond. They sought to undermine the clear moral principle by concentrating on the occasionally allowable civil action. They were less interested in Christ's explanation of God's intent than in filing the right kind of paperwork. They legitimized divorce by requiring only that the proper form be filled out.

So Jesus reemphasized God's original blueprint. "It was not this way from the beginning," He reminded them, explaining that Moses only permitted divorce because of the hardness of the people's hearts (v. 8). The Israelites knew so little of the meaning of love that divorce was allowed in order to control an increasingly chaotic situation.

Then, as now, hard hearts stem from refusing to listen to God and do what He says. Many contemporary Christians are just as deaf to God as the Old Testament Israelites. Disobedience is still at the root of many disasters in marriage.

What few people realize, however, is that divorce only *seems* to be an easy answer to the problems they face. In reality, it is never easy. Since marriage was intended to be two people becoming one, divorce is like one person becoming two. It is messy and painful. A legal document cannot cover a multitude of sins. After the agony of divorce when the harsh results of the decision are being fully comprehended, many people confess to pondering what might have happened if they had tried harder to work through the process of repentance, forgiveness, brokenness, restoration, and renewal.

IN SUMMARY

God hates divorce (Malachi 2:16). In light of this truth, we must not approach marriage with divorce as an option. When in a position to influence another person's decision, we should not be quick to counsel people toward divorce. Only when we have exhausted all paths of reconciliation should we then turn to the exception which Scripture provides.

In many cases where people casually divorce and remarry, the biblical perspective is that the new relationships are adulterous ones. The exceptions are those who divorce because of a spouse's marital unfaithfulness or, as Paul points out in 1 Corinthians 7, because a nonbelieving spouse has deserted the relationship.

It is a challenge to apply biblical teaching to the issue of divorce with careful wisdom. It's not enough for the pastor or counselor to be well versed in Scripture; he must also take into account human nature, which is eager to distort the application of Scripture to its own selfish ends. If divorce takes place apart from either of the two divinely authorized allowances, then the biblical expectation is that neither partner is free to marry another. They must either remain single or be reconciled. In contrast to today's casual attitude toward divorce, these are radical instructions to be absorbed and applied. It takes much self-control and exercise of willpower to resist society's tidal wave of relativistic thinking.

One important closing thought: The fact that an individual *may* get divorced due to one of the two biblical exceptions doesn't mean he or she *should*. Far better and more desirable is the route of repentance and reconciliation, although this option is hard after one has been betrayed by a spouse. Yet by God's grace all things are possible—even reconciliation.

Adultery is not the unforgivable sin. It is a terrible offense that inflicts emotional pain and perhaps scars, but no one should feel that his actions have placed him outside the love of God. We should be seeing far less divorce and far more reconciliation than we do within our Christian family. Society continues to be ravished by divorce and lives in the shadows of dejection, desolation, and heartache of broken relationships. The Christian community should be alive and available to provide the love and acceptance that so many wounded people have been denied.

These issues tear at the very fabric of our lives. Paul's exhortation to the Christians in Rome is vitally important for us: "Don't let the world around you squeeze you into its own mould, but let God remake you so that your whole attitude of mind is changed. Thus you will prove in practice that the will of God is good, acceptable to him and perfect" (Romans 12:2, PHILLIPS).

We need to be realistic in order to prevent marital failure. Most marriages don't disintegrate because of some bizarre event that appears like a devastating scud missile out of the blue. Much more frequently, the love in the relationship gradually evaporates like a slow leak in a tire that goes undetected for a long time. Vigilance and care are therefore necessary in the everyday events of life. Neither superficial optimism nor debilitating pessimism should permeate our thinking. We need to be realistic about the challenges, dependent upon God's resources, and committed to seeing things through to the finish.

Recent generations have grown up accustomed to unfinished projects. Young children resist cleaning their plates and tidying their rooms. Older ones find it difficult to finish homework or hold a job. Even many college graduates are finding the world a cold and difficult place, and are returning home to live with Mom and Dad again. In such a context, it is an awesome prospect to envision enjoying a relationship with another person that is only concluded by death. But that's what the Bible says, and it can be done!

CHAPTER FOUR

THE ROLE
OF A WIFE

The teaching of the Bible is radical. It is revolutionary. "Not so," say some. "It is a textbook for female subjugation, reinforcing principles that might have been all right for first-century women who apparently did not have what it takes to stand up and fight for their rights!" Such statements, while not uncommon, betray an ignorance of what the Bible actually says. The New Testament documents were revolutionary in their immediate context.

Under Jewish law a woman was a thing, the possession of her husband—along with his house, flocks, and goods. She had no legal rights. A husband could divorce his wife for any cause. Apart from the exceptions of leprosy, gross immorality, or apostasy, a wife had no right whatever to initiate divorce.

In Greek society, a respectable woman lived a life of entire seclusion. She lived in the women's apartments and did not even join her husband for meals. Complete servitude and chastity were demanded of her, but her husband could go out as much as he chose and enter into as many relationships outside marriage as he liked without incurring any stigma. The Athenian orator Demosthenes said: "We have courtesans for the sake of pleasure, we have concubines for the sake of daily cohabitation and we have wives for the purpose of having children legitimately and being faithful guardians for our household affairs."

The Roman's view of marriage was also a disaster zone. Jerome writes of one Roman woman who married her twenty-third husband—and she was the man's twenty-first wife! There was a strong feminist agenda. Women did not want to have children because they thought it spoiled their appearance. Some of them wanted to do everything men did, so they developed women wrestlers and women sword throwers. The poet and satirist Juvenal records how women began to lord it over their husbands, and then before long would vacate the home and flit from one marriage to another, "wearing out their bridal veils."

In the context of such chaos, we find the New Testament writers placing the essential dignity of women in general and wives in particular on an unshakable foundation.

> Wives, submit to your husbands as to the Lord. For the husband is the head of the wife as Christ is the head of the church, his body, of which he is the Savior. Now as the church submits to Christ, so also wives should submit to their husbands in everything . . . and the wife must respect her husband. (Ephesians 5:22–24, 33)

> Wives, in the same way be submissive to your husbands so that, if any of them do not believe the word, they may be won over without words by the behavior of their wives, when they see the purity and reverence of your lives. Your beauty should not come from outward adornment, such as braided hair and the wearing of gold jewelry and fine clothes. Instead, it should be that of your inner self, the unfading beauty of a gentle and quiet spirit, which is of great worth in God's sight. For this is the way the holy women of the past who put their hope in God used to make themselves beautiful. They were submissive to their own husbands, like Sarah, who obeyed Abraham and called him her master. You are her daughters if you do what is right and do not give way to fear. (1 Peter 3:1–6)

> Likewise, teach the older women to be reverent in the way they live, not to be slanderers or addicted to

much wine, but to teach what is good. Then they can train the younger women to love their husbands and children, to be self-controlled and pure, to be busy at home, to be kind, and to be subject to their husbands, so that no one will malign the word of God. (Titus 2:3–5)

AN OLD TESTAMENT "SUPERMODEL"

By any standards Sarai must have been beautiful. Heads turned when she entered town. She stood out from the crowd, presumably on account of her poise, elegance, bone structure, striking gaze, and the fact that her flowing robes, intended to conceal, simply enhanced her beauty. Abram recognized the peculiar prize he had in his wife. She was so attractive that she posed a threat to his security. It was quite common for a man to be killed so that his wife could become another man's wife. So when Abram and Sarai went down to Egypt, he talked her into lying about her identity ("Say you are my sister") to save his own skin. You can read the remarkable story in Genesis 12. There you will find that Sarai became the talk of the town because she was "a very beautiful woman."

Now there is no doubt that the references in Genesis to Sarai's beauty are to the physical features she possessed. But when apostle Peter refers to the Old Testament models, he says that the key to their beauty was not applied from the outside but emerged from within. Look at 1 Peter 3:1–6, quoted above. Peter invites the wives of his era to be "daughters" of Sarai, a kind of spiritual sorority, if you will, or perhaps a new breed of "supermodels," not for magazines or movies, but for displaying the beauty that accompanies those who are prepared to become a wife in the way that God's Word describes.

CULTURAL REJECTION OF THE MODEL

That standard is regarded with almost total disdain in our culture. Far more acceptable is the view expressed by Felice Swartz, president of Catalyst, writing in *Working Woman* magazine:

> By the year 2000, when the children of today's generation of career women are themselves emerging from their teens, the polarization of the sexes that put women in the home, at the nurturing end of the spectrum, and men in the office, at the work end of the spectrum, will have disappeared. And with it the stereotypes of supportive women and aggressive men.[1]

Our youngest child is in the high school graduating class of 2000, so the issues Swartz describes are not academic trifles to us but matters of practical urgency. Our "alien status" as Christians is going to be on display in family matters.

The culture may prescribe aggressive women and supportive men, and TV sitcoms may introduce lesbian or "gay" characters to their shows in an attempt to mainstream deviant behavior, but Christians are called upon to be radically different.

The woman who follows Christian standards in her behavior and beliefs will receive an unfavorable reaction from her supposedly enlightened and progressive friends. She would cause less fuss by wearing only underwear to go grocery shopping than she would by standing up for Christian principles at a wedding shower for a neighbor's daughter. In an age of personal fulfillment and assertiveness training, the Political Correctness Police will come scurrying from every corner at the mere mention of the word *submissive,* and the phrase *wives be submissive* will be a call to arms.

MALE CHAUVINISTS

It is imperative that Christians understand the instruction the Bible provides and apply it correctly to their lives. The bombastic, dictator model of male dominance finds no justification in the Bible. But the principles have been sorely misapplied in many quarters—that we must acknowledge with shame. In the seventies, Shel Silverstein captured the male chauvinist's approach in a song entitled "Put Another Log on the Fire."

Put another log on the fire
Cook me up some bacon and some beans
And go out to the car and change the tire
Wash my socks and sew my old blue jeans.

Come on, Baby.

You can fill my pipe and then go fetch my slippers
And boil me up another pot of tea
Then put another log on the fire, Babe
And come and tell me why you're leavin' me.

Now, don't I let you wash the car on Sunday?
Don't I warn you when you're gettin' fat?
Ain't I gonna take you fishin' with me someday?
Well, a man can't love a woman more than that.

Ain't I always nice to your kid sister?
Don't I take her drivin' every night?
So, sit here at my feet
'Cause I like you when you're sweet
And you know it ain't feminine to fight.

Come on, Baby.

You can fill my pipe and then go fetch my slippers
And boil me up another pot of tea
Then put another log on the fire, Babe
And come and tell me why you're leavin' me.

Those inside and outside the church who are opposed to the teaching of the Bible have attempted—with some success—to redefine *authority* as dictatorship, and *submission* as mindless subjugation. We need to retake the central ground and refuse to allow a godless culture to caricature and dismiss the timeless truth of God's Word.

WHO OWNS WHOM?

WE ARE NOT OUR OWN

Many of the arguments about who is in charge stem from a lack of understanding of first principles. A Christian couple have submission in common. Individually they do not belong to themselves—and that flies in the face of contemporary cries to "be your own person" and "look out for number one."

Although we were once foolish enough to buy into the "be your own person" jargon and were deceived by high-sounding rhetoric, when the kindness and love of God our Savior appeared, He saved us. The radical transformation brought about by His grace is seen in many ways. One of them is a change in who holds the title to our lives. Paul puts it this way at the end of 1 Corinthians 6: "You are not your own; you were bought at a price. Therefore honor God with your body."

NEITHER JEW NOR GREEK, MALE NOR FEMALE

Much marital failure can be traced to some form of identity crisis. In Galatians 3:28, Paul addresses the question of identity, saying that husband and wife share equally in the privileges of redemption: "There is neither Jew nor Greek, slave nor free, male nor female, for you are all one in Christ Jesus."

Despite the lengths to which some have gone in an attempt to use this verse as a means of overturning the rest of biblical teaching on the distinctive roles given to the husband and wife in marriage, the clear and obvious meaning of the text is this: Though there remain obvious differences between people, in spiritual matters there is to be no racial, social, or sexual discrimination. The blessings of salvation are equally shared by husband and wife.

> In recognizing believing women as the full spiritual equals of believing men, Christianity elevated women to a status they had never known before in the ancient world. In matters of rule in the home and in the church God has established the headship of men. But in the dimension of spiritual possessions and privilege there is absolutely no difference.[2]

GOD THE FATHER IS THE HEAD OF CHRIST

Yet, though there is no difference between man and woman in the nature of their salvation, there is a principle of authority in the family. Those who struggle with this concept will be helped by considering Paul's words in 1 Corinthians 11:3: "Now I want you to realize that the head of every man is Christ, and the head of the woman is man, and the head of Christ is God."

The last phrase should make us stop and think. *The head of Christ?* It sounds odd at first. After all, we know that when the Bible speaks of God the Father, the Son, and the Holy Spirit, it makes it clear that they are coequal and coeternal. Without delving into a theological discussion, it is sufficient for us to note here that God the Father is the head of Christ, not in essence or nature, but in function. For example, Christ was in very nature God but He did not cling to His privileges, but instead humbled Himself and became a servant (see Philippians 2:5–11).

THE HUSBAND IS THE HEAD OF THE WIFE

The relationship structure of Christ to God is the same one written into the fabric of marriage. The husband and wife are equal in their standing before God, and their spiritual natures are the same, *but* in order for the family to function in harmony, the woman, with no loss of dignity, takes the place of submission to the headship of her husband. God's perfect design intends that her respect, help, and obedience should be matched by her husband's servant leadership, as together they submit to the lordship of Christ. The mutuality of their relationship is clearly seen in the matter of sexual intimacy.

> The wife's body does not belong to her alone but also to her husband. In the same way, the husband's body does not belong to him alone but also to his wife. (1 Corinthians 7:4)

ADAPTING TO ONE ANOTHER

Much of the confusion surrounding this matter emerges from our inability to hold truths in balance. In stressing the necessity of submission, we fail to do service to the fact of equality. Then, when we talk about equality, we tend to pay scant attention to the nature and necessity of submission. J. B. Phillips paraphrased the concept this way: "You wives must learn to adapt yourselves to your husbands" (Ephesians 5:22, PHILLIPS). In doing so, Phillips was clearly not seeking to weaken the strength of the scriptural mandate, for later, in the same passage, he paraphrases: "The willing subjection of the Church to Christ should be reproduced in the submission of wives to their husbands" (v. 24).

But the idea of adapting is a helpful picture.

It is demanded of both parties if the marriage is to be a success. Prior to marriage the man may have been perfectly content to make unilateral decisions about everything. He may think that his taste in interior design is without parallel! But now the Lord has graciously provided him a helper, who in a whole range of aspects is clearly his superior, not least of all when it comes to decorating a house. Since she has been given to him as his helper in all things, as she adapts herself to the role God has given her, he will know the benefit.

The wife's submission is not that of a bell-hop, who waits for his name to be called and his tasks to be assigned. It is not passive, blind obedience. It is wrong to think immediately of laundry and dishes and tasks. It is right to recognize the extent of the wife's companionship and help. The ideal woman of Proverbs 31 was exceptional in her capabilities and clearly brought to the marriage key ingredients her husband could never have provided on his own.

The Bible is not implying the inferiority of women. It establishes their role as being one of honor, privilege, and necessity. The submission to which a wife is called does not negate the spiritual equality she enjoys with her husband. Every team must have a captain, and every home a leader, and God has established things in such a way that this responsibility falls to the man. His authority is limited by the broader parameters of God's Word. God never authorizes sin. So if a husband demands of his wife sinful behavior, claiming a mandate to do so on the basis of his authority, she must graciously refuse.

Some years ago I married a young couple, and, within a matter of months, the wife came to see me with a sordid tale of her husband's sexual demands. The man was clearly wrong in the things he was asking his wife to do, and, on account of his warped understanding of his role as husband, he made his wife feel that she was being less than what God expected of her. The fact was, and so often is, that God's expectations are far more sensible and reasonable than many of the unauthorized demands of selfish husbands.

We have things wrong if we imagine the scene in the Garden of Eden to be one in which Adam is lying in a hammock barking out orders to Eve about where he would like certain flowers to be planted and when he would enjoy his next cold drink. The picture is better painted in terms of his standing with a selection of plants and saying to his wife, "Eve, honey, you're far better at this stuff than me. Where do you think this should go?"

When we contemporize the picture, the girl, who when she was single, planted her yard without reference to anyone else, now finds herself adapting to this extra step and submitting to the challenges of it, because that's what God said to do. Jay Adams captured the essence of this when he wrote:

> This means if a husband's thinking is out of line, his wife's task is to help him correct his thoughts. If his life is out of line, her job is to help him return to God's path. If he simply is perplexed in a decision, she must bring her best reasons to the decision-making process. Help, given respectfully, never conflicts with submission. That is because submission requires her to contribute, to give what she has to offer. And that is what she must do, always in a spirit of respect and with a willingness to obey even if she may not agree. As a body with more than one head is a monstrosity, so too, there must be only one head to a home.[3]

WHEN CIRCUMSTANCES ARE NOT IDEAL

"That's all well and good," says a wife, "but my circumstances are far from ideal. Does all this still apply?" Often the context in which the wife finds herself is that of being married to an unbeliever. Either she married a non-Christian in the hope that he would turn around and join her (a bad strategy) or since marrying she has come to faith, apart from her husband. Or there may be cases where the wife is on the receiving end of indifference or even hostility.

The Bible addresses these circumstances in 1 Peter 3:1–6. There the apostle Peter says that it is important for the wife to learn to engage in what William Barclay called "the silent preaching of a lovely life." Her impact is going to be as a result of how she lives, not of what she says (vv. 1–2). She must trust that her husband is going to be influenced by seeing how she behaves, especially if he is unprepared to listen to what she believes.

Peter mentions two aspects of behavior. The first is *purity* (v. 2). The pagan world was focused on the externals. The first-century equivalent of shopping malls would have provided the ideal venue for "dressing to kill." The husband may well have enjoyed seeing the glances his wife received from other men as he encouraged her to dress in such a way that she was not simply attractive, but actually seductive. Now he notices that though she has not become drab, she has begun to express herself more modestly. Her behavior makes him think.

At the same time, and linked with purity, is *reverence* (v. 2). The significant truth about a Christian woman's relationship to her husband is that it mirrors her relationship to the Lord. There is no possibility of a married woman's surrender to a heavenly Christ that is not made visible and actual by her submission to her earthly husband. When you hear a child speak disparagingly to his father, there's a fair chance he has heard his mother do the same. Listen to a daughter cross-question her dad in public and you have an inkling of the approach taken by her mother in the home. If the most important thing a man can do for his children is to love their mother sacrificially, then the most important thing a mother can do for her children is to respect their father.

Peter brings up Sarah, our "supermodel," to make the point. Peter says of Sarah that she "obeyed Abraham and called him her master" (v. 6). The reference Peter is making is to Genesis 18:12, where in talking to herself Sarah spoke of her husband with this expression of reverence. What we think or say privately is usually a good indicator of how we really feel about things. So, in her heart of hearts, Sarah respected her husband, not because he was "the best" or "never put a foot wrong," but because God had placed him in a position of authority as head of the home.

In Peter's exhortation, the plan is this: The husband sees an outward change as a result of an inward transformation he cannot see and probably does not understand. In a whole series of contrasts he makes the point. Outward beauty versus inward beauty. External attachments versus internal attitudes. Changing fashions versus unfading beauty.

Through these contrasts he is led quietly to the Christ his wife honors (vv. 1–6).

UNFADING BEAUTY

These are matters of pressing urgency. Women are not exclusively, but they are particularly, bombarded by the mentality of the mall. Hair, clothes, jewelry, and the potential enslavement to fashion calls out to them from the newsstands, radio commercials, and television advertising. So, as husbands, we need to learn to praise our wives and daughters for inner loveliness, lest by default, if not by design, we set them on a quest for beauty that will inevitably and ultimately not be fulfilled.

A wife is to ensure that irrespective of what she may have in her jewelry box, she is cultivating "the unfading beauty of a gentle and quiet spirit" (1 Peter 3:4). This should not be misunderstood to be referring to a certain kind of personality. Gregarious or quiet, funny or serious, extrovert or introvert, the qualities of a gentle and quiet spirit will shine through. Nor are these gems to be confused with natural timidity, or uneasy reserve, or affected piety. They are expressions of spiritual fruit.

NOT GIVING WAY TO FEAR

For a woman to be part of this spiritual sorority will demand that she "not give way to fear" (1 Peter 3:6). The Bible tells us that "perfect love casts out fear" (1 John 4:18, NKJV). The wife is not to be prevented from doing what is right because she is afraid of social disapproval. It is tempting to capitulate and fit in rather than stand boldly out of reverence for God. So strong is the pressure, Christians who face disapproval, especially in the realm of academia, may feel that they must marry the spirit of the age and prepare for widowhood in a subsequent generation.

I have the strongest admiration for my Orthodox Jewish friends who continue to live by their convictions, refusing to be intimidated by the changing theological fashions of the time. They are convinced that tradition has taught them who they are and what God expects of them and so they live. If only we as Christians were marked by such boldness, not least of all in this crucial realm of marriage—God's way.

"ELDER" WOMEN HELPING THE YOUNGER

I fully understand when a wife says to me, "I have read about being a wife and mother. What I need now are some examples." The Bible recognizes this, and that is why in Titus 2:3–5 older women are called to be illustrations of those principles to those who are younger.

What, then, is the magic age at which a woman

qualifies as "older"? The fact is that to some degree every woman is an older woman. The college student is able to model the principle of purity in dating to the high school teenager who looks up to her. The young married girl can help and encourage the younger friend who has questions about when to say "I do." The mother of three teenage children can certainly have an impact on the young wife with toddlers, and the empty-nest mother can prepare the generation behind her for the avenue into which they are about to walk.

Central to all of this is a personal, growing faith and trust in the Lord Jesus that is not always related to chronology. There may be far more spiritual maturity and wisdom in a young woman who has soaked up God's Word than in an older woman who has simply played around on the fringes. In short, there is no reason to try to create hard and fast categories of who the older women are. The process is straightforward enough. Those who have run a few more laps can help the other women as some of them set out on the marathon of marriage and motherhood.

MOTHERHOOD AND
THE STRESSES OF MARRIAGE

Motherhood is a high calling, and parenting brings with it peculiar joys and privileges—but those blessings can also bring challenges that test the breaking points on the rope that binds husband and wife. In the routine of the everyday housewife, there is great potential for marital failure.

Consider the trip to the grocery store a young mother makes. Do you see her face as she juggles her youngster in the makeshift chair in the front of her cart or as she calls out to her toddler, who has decided to rearrange the cereal boxes? Right about now, she probably thinks, her husband will have concluded the morning session at the regional sales conference and will be getting ready for an afternoon on the golf course. Fighting back a rising tide of resentment and feeling guilty about her daydreams, she heads down the frozen food aisle on her way to the checkout. As she buckles the children into their seats in the minivan, she is probably not thinking about her role in terms of a sacred duty. Erma Bombeck expressed these sentiments in this way:

> It hits on a dull, overcast Monday morning. I awake realizing there is no party in sight for the weekend, I'm out of bread, and I've got a dry skin problem. So I say it aloud to myself, "What's a nice girl like me doing in a dump like this?"
>
> The draperies are dirty (and will disintegrate if laundered), the arms of the sofa are coming through.

There is Christmas tinsel growing out of the carpet. And some clown has written in the dust on the coffee table, YANKEE GO HOME.

It's those rotten kids. It's their fault I wake up feeling so depressed. If only they'd let me wake up in my own way. Why do they have to line up along my bed and stare at me like Moby Dick just washed up on a beach somewhere?[4]

To whatever degree this represents the intermittent feelings of the average mother, we need to pay careful attention to what the Bible has to say about these issues.

CULTURAL CONFUSION OVER MOTHERHOOD

It certainly doesn't help matters that so much around us in movies and magazines and the choices of our friends tends to challenge and undermine the unique place of motherhood—even to the extent of declaring that the role has little to do with gender. It doesn't matter who the "mom" is. It can be dad—after all, wasn't that what *Mr. Mom* was suggesting?

There is no doubt that a husband is capable of doing far more in the nurturing process of children than he usually does or should do, but that does not provide us with a basis for reversing the roles. The fact that it is the mother's body which produces all the necessary nourishment for the infant's life is viewed as nothing more than an evolutionary happenstance and certainly not the work of an infinite creator God. These views have been clearly expressed in the literature of the last twenty-five years. Indeed, as in other eras, Christians failed to read the writing on the wall in the seventies, and now we find ourselves scrambling in the nineties.

Jessie Bernard's book *The Future of Marriage* was described as "an ultra-provocative forecast of the psychological, political, social and economic state of women in the next generation." In it, she wrote:

> What we see today is the tail-end of a comet, the tail of a model of motherhood that began to disintegrate when it struck the twentieth century.
>
> Our society is engaged in rewriting the script for the role of women as mothers. This is no side-show, no minor concern. . . . It is the heart of the matter, one of the most momentous projects, relevant for the future of our species.[5]

Tragically, in too many pews and from too many pulpits there is emerging a growing army of chocolate soldiers who are melting in the heat of these attacks. In attempting to appear "culturally sophisticated," we have absorbed more godless thinking than we realize. Walter J. Chantry addresses this when he writes:

Our generation has highlighted the oppression of women. The symptoms are not difficult to identify. Women have too often been held in contempt. Large numbers of them have been subjected to verbal, social and physical abuses. Women's magazines and social activists have pointed the finger at very serious ill-treatments which subject multitudes to misery.

Our world has little difficulty describing the quandary of women. But it has completely mistaken the root cause. Consequently, women are being offered a faulty solution to their real troubles. False diagnosis usually leads to improper measures of correction. In this case the cure proposed by the world simply compounds female misery.[6]

TEACHING *ABOUT* THE HOME *IN* THE HOME

In the Bible, the role of a wife and mother is not left to conjecture, as if we could put it together like a neighborhood quilting project—each person showing up with her own fabric and adding her own square. It is not treated as a matter of personal preference. It is clearly established and unfolded from the first book on. As we have seen, by the time of the New Testament, Jesus, and in turn the apostles, were challenging the repressive and chauvinistic tendencies of Roman, Greek, and Judaistic cultures.

The verses from Titus 2 discussed earlier concerning the vital importance of younger women being influenced by those for whom the years have brought experience, sympathy, and understanding apply as much to mothers as they do to wives. And it would seem obvious that the context in which Paul envisages this taking place is the home. I do not think that he imagined a new breed of women teachers standing behind podiums and providing lists of material to be stored in the three-ring binders of the young mothers who have left home to attend "class."

That is not to say that such an approach is wrong or doesn't work. It is to say that I believe the apostle would be surprised to see the way in which we tend to apply these verses. The influence of the older on the younger is apparently natural, spontaneous, and unprogrammed—taking place around a crib rather than in a class; at a sink rather than a study; in a nursery, not a seminary. When I return to the United Kingdom and stay in my sisters' homes, it is striking to see the similarity that exists between how my mother did things and how they do them. Despite the fact that our mother died when they were just young girls, the influence of her example was already stamped upon them for good. She left behind the lasting impression that there can be no greater task, no higher calling in all the world, than to make a home.

SUMMING IT UP:
PRIORITIES FROM TITUS 2:4–5

One reason cracks appear in the foundation of a marriage is the absence of agreed-upon responsibilities or failure to maintain a commitment to the basics.

A husband must recognize that for his wife to bring all her intellect and talent and wisdom and creativity to bear upon the task of raising godly sons and daughters is to commit herself to a job description of nerve-jangling dimensions. It is therefore imperative that wives know that their husbands share their vision, applaud their efforts, are in awe of their abilities, and are humbled by their selflessness.

There won't be a day that passes, when from some source, the temptation to capitulate to a secular model will present itself. *Is this really significant?* the wife says to herself, as she packs the 5,129th school lunch. *After all, Stephanie, down the street, has the fun of travel and the chance to meet all kinds of people, working as she does in sales.* The husband needs to be at hand to affirm his wife by reminding her that God has assigned a nobler work to women than merely to parallel men's activities.

"TO LOVE THEIR HUSBANDS AND CHILDREN" (V. 4)

In Ephesians 5:25, husbands are directed to love their wives. In Titus 2:4, we are told that it is important that wives be taught to love their husbands and children. Does that not strike you as strange? *Taught* to love? "I thought" says a young wife, "that you either felt it for him or you didn't. But I never ever considered being taught to love him." This kind of response indicates how heavily we have come to rely on the notion of romantic love as the basis for our marriage relationship.

That is why it is so important for a young woman who is struggling with this to have someone explain to her the huge difference between the superficial philosophy of marriage, available at the checkout counter, and the practical instruction of God's Word. How liberating for her to understand that her feelings of frustration and emotional low tide are actually quite natural and have been experienced by many before her—and this will not be the last time she feels this way. Finding herself in this emotional desert, she must be warned against thinking that she could quench her thirst by a "real job." She needs to know it is a mirage.

Let's be as honest as we can. Husbands are not always the most attractive and lovable objects. How are wives supposed to love someone who rises before dawn, leaves in the darkness, fails to call during the day, arrives home exhausted, eats dinner without expressing appreciation, falls asleep in front of the TV, and then stands up suddenly to announce his departure for bed—for, after all, "I have an early start tomorrow."

Now there are multiple issues in this scenario that need to be addressed. But given that such a picture is not uncommon, the wife is in need of help so that she can learn what it means to love in that context.

And what of the children? Does a mother really need to be taught to love her children? Apparently so. They can test the limits of her patience, and regularly do. Their rooms can be as untidy as their attitudes are bad. She can wonder why after all those early years of teaching them the necessity of courtesy they can answer the phone as they do. What does it mean to love them when they are apparently nothing more than a means of testing her sanctification? A mother's love for her children is not to be, says Matthew Henry, "a fond foolish love, neglecting due reproof and correction, but a regular Christian love, forming their life and manners aright, taking care of their souls as well as their bodies."

When the husband is insensitive to all his wife is going through in these times, when his best attempt at encouragement is to say "Get over it," he may unwittingly be opening the door for his wife to establish an emotional attachment with someone other than her husband. She may not even be thinking of it in those terms when the sensitive young man in their Bible study group shows an interest in her stressed-out state and promises to pray for her. When he calls during the week "just to see how you are doing," she may be left reflecting on how nice it is to have that kind of attention, especially in the absence of her workaholic spouse.

It is difficult to overstate the necessity of partnership and mutual support between husband and wife in the establishing of these priorities. Barnes, writing in an earlier generation, said: "Mutual love between a husband and wife will diffuse comfort through the obscurest cottage of poverty, the want of it cannot be supplied by all that can be furnished in the palaces of the great." It is surely never too late for a refresher course in the emotional, mental, spiritual, and physical aspects of married love.

"TO BE SELF-CONTROLLED AND PURE" (V. 5)

Self-control and purity are required of all Christians, and yet here they are highlighted as vital ingredients in the recipe for being a successful wife and mother. The challenge to be self-controlled in a world that is increasingly out of control is very real. In the management of the home, the wife must exercise financial control. In some cases, she will be better suited to the matters of finance than her husband, and he will have confidence in her judgment. Others will need to be under the supervision of their husbands. Whatever the degree of freedom a wife may enjoy in financial matters, she is to exercise self-control. This will probably mean developing the reflex action of dumping offers of credit in the garbage. It will mean resisting the temptation to borrow from next month to take care of today. In certain cases, it will mean learning to harness the temptation to purchase things on impulse, especially when the demands of the children become loud and insistent.

For some, the matter of self-control will have particular application to eating habits. I was recently with a family friend who confided in me that she had unwittingly grown dependent upon coffee. Throughout the day, from her first waking moment, she had a cup in her hand or close at hand. Added to that, she began to snack constantly, and before she knew it, she had become significantly heavier than she had ever been. Eventually she recognized the application of Paul's words: "'Everything is permissible for me'—but I will not be mastered by anything" (1 Corinthians 6:12). She made it a matter of prayer and has gained victory over what had become a real problem and over which she was unable to exercise self-control.

Another area that represents a problem for some women is that of tidiness and the upkeep of the home. We all understand when the pressures of other things take precedence over the vacuuming and dusting and tidying, for a while. Everyone experiences that. However, for some, the absence of self-discipline in forming and executing a plan of action has resulted in their homes becoming an embarrassment to themselves, and certainly to their families. It is not extreme to ensure that the beds are made, the dishwasher loaded (or emptied), and the laundry brought under manageable control before a woman dashes off for social events or exercise or hair care or whatever. When she sees these things as just a chore—a drag on her energy—she will be tempted to neglect them. But when she sees them as an expression of glory to God, then the most menial task is transformed.

Each family will have its own way of handling these aspects of life, but there is little doubt that the wife has a key role in establishing the guidelines for order. Practical areas in which this matter of self-control is relevant are many. I have probably dabbled more than is wise. I leave it here!

But what of purity? Clearly, Paul must have had certain circumstances in mind when he mentioned this. When he instructs Timothy about the conduct of women within his church, he tells the young pastor that he wants the women "to dress modestly, with decency and propriety" (1 Timothy 2:9). As we have previously noted, it is one thing for a woman to make herself attractive and another for her to make herself look seductive. Women know the difference and so do men. It will not do for women to parade themselves in such a way as to derive gratification from the obvious visual impact they are making on the opposite sex.

But purity is first of all a matter of the mind. That some women are in the grip of godless soap operas is clear from their own admission. That is a trap from which they need to be extricated. In the same way, certain books and magazines do not contribute to the development of purity and are therefore to be avoided at all costs. These radical priorities are in order that we might learn to live as lights in the middle of a crooked and perverse generation.

"TO BE BUSY AT HOME, TO BE KIND" (V. 5)

Here the emphasis is clearly upon the unique prerogative of a mother in relation to home life.

There is possibly no single area of family matters over which more battles continue to be fought than the issue of working mothers. As an unashamed fan of *The Waltons* and *Little House on the Prairie,* I freely confess my nostalgic longings after the clarity and simplicity of such times. When dads were tough and mothers cooked and cleaned. When girls were feminine and played with dolls, and boys learned to chop wood and haul water and prepared for manhood.

The contemporary chaos in which differences between the genders are being increasingly blurred, accompanied by disdain for the idea that there would ever be distinctive roles for men and women, makes this period in many respects not a happy time in which to live. The fact that I am not alone in this feeling can be deduced from the wide appeal of such movies as *Sense and Sensibility, Jane Eyre,* and *Emma.* In each case, the film portrays a worldview that appeals to everything honest and pure and right within a man and a woman. The films do not depict perfection, nor are they without fault, but they are to be preferred far above much that is offered today.

Contemporary fiction and academic treatises constantly convey the idea that there should be no distinction in roles between men and women. Indeed, we are told, if women were truly emancipated from male dominance we could look forward to a bright tomorrow. This is a total contradiction of what the Bible teaches.[7]

The unique role of motherhood does not simply last nine months. Failure to grasp this fact has generated day-care centers, maternity leave, and an almost frantic obsession on the part of many women to ensure that having done all "the hard work" of conceiving, carrying, and delivering the child, they can quickly get back to their "real calling," which, they believe, gives them significance.

On two occasions in the past ten years, I have had to get a new barber on account of this. The first time this happened, my hairdresser, a woman named Bobby, informed me that she would be taking a short break from her duties so that she could have her baby. But, she assured me, she would be back in a matter of weeks, if all went well. "Going well" involved finding day care for her infant so that she could cut hair!

When I asked her why she would not just hang up her shears and be a mom, she was indignant. Working had little to do with money. Her husband was well paid and they were not in need of a second paycheck. It was, she told me, because she did not want to become "one of those women who sits around the house in the middle of the morning still in her robe and with nothing to do but take care of the infant's input and output."

No amount of encouragement from me could help her see that she had bought the stereotype created by feminism. She was clearly annoyed when I told her that despite how much I had come to rely upon her expertise in cutting my hair, she had just cut it for the last time—for I would not contribute in any way to her neglecting her baby, which I believed she was about to do so that she could cut hair!

The second occasion followed the earlier pattern, although I am thrilled to report that, in the case of Vivienne, she did not return to work but settled in to the higher calling of being a wife and mother.

A few summers ago, I was speaking at a conference center on Lake Michigan and, in the course of my remarks, made a strong statement concerning women who would neglect the responsibilities of mothering to "poke around in other people's mouths, fulfilling the role of a dental hygienist." On the following day, when I arrived at the podium, a letter was waiting for me, which read as follows:

Dear Alistair,
"Remember now thy dental hygienist in the days of thy youth, before the day comes when thou shalt say:

'I have no need of her,'" due to the fact that you didn't have your teeth cleaned and the grinders have ceased because they are few!

As our motto states, *carpe diem* (seize the day) or *carpe dentura* (seize your dentures). The choice is yours.

With all due respect,

Your dental hygienist

P.S. We "love those who thunder out the Word" (George Whitfield). Keep Thundering!

Now I include this letter not to take up space and certainly not to make light of the point under consideration. I do so because it makes another point. The writer of that note was in no doubt as to the strength of my conviction regarding working mothers. But she recognized what I understand, namely, that while we can be forceful when it comes to laying down the biblical principle, at the point of specific application we need to exercise particular care. Although I have concluded that it is safe to infer from the biblical text that it is not right for a wife to work outside the home, when a woman has the primary financial responsibility for raising preschool and school age children, I recognize I cannot be dogmatic about it, since the Scriptures are not.

Clearly, the single mother has few options open to her apart from working outside the home. But, at the same time, I have little doubt that Christian businessmen could become far more creative and less demanding in making it possible for women in such circumstances to be relieved of their responsibilities in time to be home when the children arrive. Where computer technology allows for working from home, that should be encouraged.

Some couples have put themselves in such a financial bind that the wife is working to ensure their survival. The larger question of financial self-control needs to be addressed and a speedy plan of resolution put in place so as to allow the wife to return to the home.

Some wives may have peculiar problems with loneliness which they counteract by involvement in the workplace. There are doubtless other creative ways in which this issue could be addressed, if they so choose.

There are all kinds of exceptions we could offer for consideration. But at the heart of the matter is the question: What is involved in motherhood? When our answer is in the spirit of the quote below, we quickly see that leaving our children in a nursery in exchange for fulfilling this role is a grave mistake. Walter J. Chantry observes:

> What is involved in motherhood? After birth pangs bring children into this world there come years of life pangs. It is a mother's task and privilege to oversee the

forging of a personality in her sons and daughters. For this she must set a tone in the home which builds strong character. Hers is to take great Christian principles and practically apply them in every-day affairs —doing it simply and naturally. It is her responsibility to analyze each child mentally, physically, socially, spiritually. Talents are to be developed, virtues must be instilled, faults are to be patiently corrected, young sinners are to be evangelized. She is building men and women for God. Results may not be possible until she has labored for fifteen or twenty years. Even when her task ends, the true measure of her work awaits the full maturity of her children. Moses would be much more than an Egyptian rebel and an obscure shepherd, but Jochebed (his mother) would not live to observe the consequences of her motherhood.[8]

What mother, reading that, does not find herself pausing in earnest prayer, that she might even approximate to such a standard. And in it all she is to show kindness. How practical! The demands of the journey through this often difficult terrain may squeeze out the last of our human kindness. There will be times, more than we wish, when our wife's battery is running low and we must become, under God, the source of replenishment, emotionally and practically.

"TO BE SUBJECT TO THEIR HUSBANDS" (V. 5)

We have dealt with this elsewhere. We might

simply note here that to live as God intends without paying heed to this is not difficult—it's *impossible!*

The chaos and confusion that surround too many marriages can be traced to the simple fact that couples have chosen to tamper with the directions. It will only be when they admit their total dependence upon the wisdom of God's Word and the power of God's Spirit that they will get back on track.

"SO THAT NO ONE WILL MALIGN THE WORD OF GOD" (V. 5)

Paul states that the purpose in all of this is that we be good advertisements for the Christian faith. Our friends and neighbors will judge our doctrine by its practical effect upon our daily lives. If, when they are in our homes, they encounter a dimension that cannot be explained in human terms, then both we and they are on to something. When marriages work as God intends, they act as magnets, drawing the disillusioned and confused to consider the reality of Christian faith. Here we have one of the greatest opportunities to show the difference Jesus makes in our hearts and in our homes: not in producing perfect children; not in being perfect wives, or perfect mothers, or perfect husbands. Instead, being honest enough to admit our defeats, acknowledge our struggles, and affirm our dependence upon the Lord Jesus.

CHAPTER FIVE

THE ROLE
OF A HUSBAND

Now we have come to the hard part! As I mentioned before, when I started the text that has become this book, I did not set out to add to the vast collection of books on this subject. I was simply writing a memo to myself to help me guard against becoming part of the sorry statistics of marital failure. Apart from spiritual shipwrecks—the professions of faith in Christ that have run aground on the rocks of rebellion and confusion—nothing pains me more than to watch as husbands and wives break up on the sea of life.

MARITAL SHIPWRECKS

Each of us can recall the streets and avenues down which we used to walk in our younger days.

We were enchanted by the lights in the windows, the signs of life on the porch, and the obvious care that had been taken in the yard. But today, that is all just a memory. The families have moved away, the buildings are about to be demolished, and any voices raised in protest have long since been silenced.

In much the same way, each of us can think of avenues of life filled with happy families. We enjoyed their company, learned from their example, and wanted to be like them one day. Then, to our great surprise, these shining lights began to dim, and today there's not a flicker left of the love and romance and laughter and faithfulness that once made these homes so attractive.

Yes, and too many of these are the marriages of Christian leaders. Since coming to the United States in 1983, my heart has ached as authors of books on marital bliss have had to acknowledge their own crumbling relationships. They were aware of the biblical instruction—indeed, they had enjoyed the privilege of sharing their insights with others—yet today they are better known for their failures than for all the guidelines to marital success they once offered.

For all who walk away, never to return, there is a large crowd of couples whose marriages are held together by chewing gum and string. Or, to mix a metaphor, they are like the streets on a Hollywood movie set that look great from the front, but 'round back, there's nothing there. The part displayed to the public is held together by ropes and pulleys and could be dismantled in a moment.

Held together by custom, convention, and the fear of what their friends at church would think if they broke up, these couples endure a pale imitation of what marriage is meant to be. They have grown accustomed to sleeping separately and planning their agendas in isolation. Civility and obligation have long since replaced passion and commitment. Like individuals who see physical symptoms but refuse to be checked out by a doctor, lest their fears are proved to be justified, they hide until the disease has become so invasive that healing will demand a miracle. Of course, that is just what we might expect when we come to a God who is able to do far more than we can ask or even imagine (Ephesians 3:20)!

None of these people set out on the journey with the thought of running aground. They all thought they would be successful. Thus it seems only sensible to try to learn from their mistakes and failures, so as to keep from repeating their folly. While I do not live paralyzed by fear in relation to these things, I *do* want to take Paul's exhortation seriously: "So let the man who feels sure of his standing today be careful that he does not fall tomorrow" (1 Corinthians 10:12, PHILLIPS).

TAKING CARE OF WHAT WE LOVE

As I write about the responsibility of husbands, the words of James ring in my ears: "Not many of you should presume to be teachers, my brothers, because you know that we who teach will be judged more strictly" (James 3:1). I want to write about these issues with the same humble spirit that should mark any attempt to share one's faith—the excitement of one beggar telling another beggar where to find food.

Men must resist the cultural tendency to rate image higher than character. It is all too easy to content ourselves with keeping up an image while neglecting the essential disciplines that forge our characters. When we expose ourselves to the searchlight of God's Word, there will be no room for pretense. As a husband and father, I am forced to recognize that "if Christianity doesn't work at home, then it doesn't work!"

The Bible is clear in declaring that if a man cannot take care of his own home, then he has no business endeavoring to take care of the church:

> Husbands, love your wives, just as Christ loved the church and gave himself up for her to make her holy,

cleansing her by the washing with water through the word, and to present her to himself as a radiant church, without stain or wrinkle or any other blemish, but holy and blameless. In this same way, husbands ought to love their wives as their own bodies. He who loves his wife loves himself. After all, no one ever hated his own body, but he feeds and cares for it, just as Christ does the church—for we are members of his body. "For this reason a man will leave his father and mother and be united to his wife, and the two will become one flesh." This is a profound mystery —but I am talking about Christ and the church. However, each one of you also must love his wife as he loves himself, and the wife must respect her husband. (Ephesians 5:25–33)

Have you noticed how fanatical some men become over their cars? They wash, polish, and pamper them almost continually. They drive them sparingly. They service them regularly to ensure they remain in tip-top shape. They don't like other people tampering with them. In public, a man may refer to his vehicle as his "little beauty," but he may also have a special name for his car known only to himself and the automobile!

These guys love to be seen in their cars, hoping to attract admiring glances. They can talk about them for hours, having memorized the details of the handbook. They park them in the remote corners of the parking lot to prevent dents from less concerned motorists.

I'm sure you're already ahead of me. Many of the men I have just described give more time and attention to the machines in their garages than to the women in their living rooms. Overstated? Probably, but it is essential not to miss the point: *The enjoyment we derive from something is directly related to the time and trouble we take to nurture and care for it.*

I'm not suggesting that men treat their wives like cars! But I want to emphasize that when a man proves himself capable of displaying tender care toward his toys, he has no excuse when it comes to his relationships. It just doesn't work when he tries to justify apathy toward his wife by claiming, "I'm just not put together that way."

NOT THE EASIER ROLE

It is fairly common to hear people suggest that within marriage the husband has been given "the easy part of the deal." Many men are quick to quote the passages discussed in chapter 4 regarding headship, authority, and the obligation for women to submit to their husbands. But they don't seem as eager to recall Ephesians 5:25–33 (quoted above) or the admonition earlier in Ephesians 5 to "submit to one another out of reverence for Christ" (v. 21).

Whenever I hear a husband "remind" his wife about his authority and her duty to submit, I know he is someone who does not understand the reciprocal nature of submission within marriage. Truth decay is already at work in such a marriage and will need to be drilled out and repaired if further deterioration is to be prevented. Scripture provides no basis for concluding that all the privileges of marriage accrue to the husband while all the obligations fall to the wife. There is no doubt that some couples live as if that were the case, but such faulty thinking is in need of correction.

If a husband starts believing that his is the easier role in the marriage relationship, he should consider what it means to "love your wife, just as Christ loved the church." While human men cannot match the *degree* of love Jesus displays (since His love is divine and infinite), they are to love in the same *manner.* Christ initiated love for the church, and His love remains constant regardless of the response He receives.

TAKING THE INITIATIVE IN NURTURING LOVE

Similarly, the husband has the responsibility of initiating, nurturing, and maintaining love within the marriage. The leadership vacuum within so many homes is largely due to the husband's lack of initiative in providing love for his wife. In far too many cases the wife has assumed the initiating role, not because she wants the position, but because she is afraid that the car is about to careen off the road, since her husband has vacated the seat or has fallen asleep at the wheel. A staggering number of men have gone AWOL when it comes to this. Whenever a wife is longing for companionship and intimacy elsewhere, the problem can usually be traced to the husband's unwillingness to take the initiative in providing love.

EXERCISING SACRIFICIAL LOVE

The love of a husband for his wife is also to be marked by sacrifice. Jesus gave Himself up for the church, not on the basis of the attractiveness of those who became the objects of His love, but on account of His grace. God loves because it is His nature to do so, and He has poured out His love into our hearts so that our love will be different from that of the world.

Our culture perceives love in terms of a response to something regarded as attractive or meaningful. Love continues as long as those characteristics are in place, but fades with the loss of the physical appeal of the object or person. In contrast, Christian love is to extend far beyond the boundaries of appearance and personality.

DWELLING ACCORDING TO KNOWLEDGE

In addition to Paul's instructions to husbands, Peter has a challenge as well:

> Husbands, in the same way be considerate as you live with your wives, and treat them with respect as the weaker partner and as heirs with you of the gracious gift of life, so that nothing will hinder your prayers. (1 Peter 3:7)

What does Peter mean when he calls husbands to "be considerate as you live with your wives"? Is he simply reminding men to be courteous—not to interrupt and finish her sentences for her, to hold the door open, to stand up when she comes into the room? These matters are trivial in light of the far-reaching instruction he has just given to the wives (1 Peter 3:1–6). So what is at the heart of this exhortation?

The literal translation is this: "Husbands, likewise dwell together according to knowledge." The context of this statement is important. Peter has previously observed that before we were converted we lived in ignorance and followed our own evil desires (1 Peter 1:14). But as we experience new life in Christ, that previous way of living changes. Our thinking is now conforming to a different standard. Pagan lust is replaced by Christian love.

Previously we may have had the same outlook on marriage as any man on the street, but now our marriage relationships are raised to the standards set forth in the truth of Scripture. Therefore, we can live with our wives in the *knowledge* of the wonderful provisions God has made for us. We have *knowledge* of the clear parameters that God has established for marriage, so we can enjoy the unique purposes He has ordained for us as husbands and wives. In the *knowledge* of what our wives are by nature and by grace, our treatment of them should be marked by gentleness and honor.

DEMONSTRATING RESPECT

When I listen to a wife describe her husband's diminishing care for her, she will often cry as she contrasts the early days with the current experience. The common story goes something like this: "When we were dating, and at the beginning of our marriage, my husband would watch out for me. I felt secure in his attention and affection. Now he usually ignores me, and I have no sense that he respects me at all. At office functions, he puts on a good show and introduces me around, but I am very quickly forgotten as he impresses the crowd with his stories. When we get home, he is full and I am empty. Yet he is so insensitive that he doesn't even notice."

This absence of honor and respect will often be seen in the way the children treat their mother. While they have the capacity for disrespect without any coaching from their dad, the fact remains that the way in which a son addresses his mother will often be a direct reflection of the attitude of the husband for his wife.

THE TREASURE OF A WIFE

There is no more precious gift entrusted to a man than the treasure of his wife. She is to be admired and prized above all others. She is to have first place in his heart, mind, and affections. She is to be given special care and attention that leaves no doubt of her husband's esteem. This is even more essential when women find themselves under severe attack for attempting to fulfill the biblical mandates for the role of wife and mother. As a woman invests her life in motherhood and lives in submission to a less than perfect (often unbearable) husband, she may be bombarded by the taunting barbs of peers, who mock such a "medieval approach" to life.

Husbands should put themselves in the place of the wife who told me of spending the afternoon with a group of neighborhood ladies. She went home recalling discussions about sexual fantasies and materialistic desires. She also was still recoiling from the scornful responses she had received for expressing her opinions about marriage. She had told the group she believed her identity was to be found in communion with her husband and not in competition. They had howled derisively at that one. She had also explained that there was more involved in a woman taking her husband's last name than was often thought.

Now she is home, battle-scarred and weary, hovering over the stove, trying yet again to time the meal for the unannounced arrival of her husband. She hopes that when he gets home she will have her emotional batteries recharged. She is looking to her husband to provide affirmation, approval, affection, and maybe even one of those good back rubs.

Then he walks in, late, tired, and inconsiderate. Talked out, he simultaneously picks up the mail and reaches for the TV remote. She watches him eat and winces inwardly as he announces the racquetball match that awaits him. Two hours later he reappears, and she knows better than to expect anything other than the sound of the shower, the sweaty togs in the laundry room, and maybe an "I'm sorry"—and good night.

That night, as she lies staring at the cracks on the ceiling, she must be very careful in case she allows the suggestions of the neighborhood wives earlier that day to find a lodging place in a corner of her mind.

There is no excuse for the behavior of the husband in this scenario. His behavior has one word written all over it—selfishness. Yet numerous women can tell stories like it—and worse. A fit of remorse on the husband's part may produce flowers and "out to dinner," but if he continues on a regular basis to disregard his wife's needs and God's command, the special evenings will have quickly diminishing returns and the weeds he is choosing to ignore will turn his garden into a jungle.

Some husbands want to defend themselves. They come to me from time to time when the discussion centers on the wife's "headache syndrome." It seems to them that their wives do not share their interest in physical intimacy. This complaint seems more common among husbands who have been married for a number of years. In the majority of instances, the husband is badly off the mark. He wants to talk about enforcing his headship, defining the extent of his rule, and giving the wife some pointers on submission. The husband is always visibly shaken when I tell him his primary goal is to love his wife—not to enforce any of the aspects he is attempting to single out. Often the husband fails to see that he is so focused on *getting* that he has lost the joy and fulfillment found in *giving.* The progression almost always runs along these lines: no meaningful communication . . . no tenderness . . . no understanding . . . no sweetness . . . no listening . . . no sensitivity . . . no response . . . *no wonder!*

THE WEAKER PARTNER

The honor a husband is to bestow upon his wife is directly related to who she is naturally and spiritually. Peter calls her the *weaker* partner—not the *weak* partner. This is very important. Peter has already established the fact of human frailty, which pertains to both husband and wife (1 Peter 1:24). So both husband and wife are weak, but of the two, the wife is the weaker.

Peter is not making a derogatory statement or suggesting the wife's inferiority. Most likely he is referring to physical constitution, for other Scriptures do not allow us to apply the statement to mental or moral capacity. Yet feminists attack Peter's statement because they see it used as a tool employed by men to keep women subjugated. Behind their agenda is usually a worldview that rejects God as Creator. Consequently, mankind is perceived simply as a form of turbocharged monkey with no significant gender differences and certainly no distinctive roles. Such ideas are nonsense.

While I am prepared to freely admit that there are times when Sue can get the top off the relish jar and I can't, and while I know that she is smarter than me in many areas and endures physical pain without undue complaint, unlike me, the exceptions do not alter the rule. The tennis matches at Wimbledon are divided by gender because of the strength and power difference that remains between the sexes. The ladies' tees at golf may not be required by an exceptionally few long-hitting ladies, but by and large they are a rightful accommodation to the discrepancy that remains between men and women in the length of their drives.

In an earlier age, when people had a God-centered view of the world, there was nothing demeaning to women in the recognition of this aspect of their femininity. Now, in our postmodern world, the women dig the roads, while men become cosmetic technicians; and girls play with trucks, while boys play with dolls—and we are asked to call it progress. There is no need to apologize for the Bible. It is trustworthy at all points, not least of all in its recognition of the differences between the sexes which God ordained.

Having said all that, another possible explanation for Peter's reference to the "weaker partner" has been offered. In this view, Peter is referring to the fact that, by marrying, the wife has accepted a position of submission and therefore vulnerability. Consequently, the husband is commanded not to take advantage of her or to exploit her "weakness" in God's design.

In either interpretation, it is important that the husband not overburden his wife or prevent her from exercising her talents. Some wives testify to "feeling useless" for no other reason than the husband's failure to create an environment in which she can flourish. In the partnership of marriage, delegation is not downward; it is lateral.

HEIRS TOGETHER OF
THE GRACIOUS GIFT OF LIFE

The distinctions that exist physically do not apply spiritually. The wife believes in the same Savior, is redeemed by the same ransom, lives by the same grace, and looks forward to the same destiny as her believing husband.

In all the remarkable dimensions of marriage for the Christian, surely none is more amazing than this: That this girl who is my earthly treasure and physical companion is also related to me at an even more significant level. She is my sister in Christ. When in heaven there is no marriage and our earthly ties are severed, we will still enjoy a union that is eternal in its significance. Throughout all eternity we will be able to unite our voices in praise and adoration of the One who not only created us and granted us the unbelievable joy of earthly companionship, but far more, "raised us up with Christ and seated us with him in the heavenly realms in Christ Jesus, in order that in the coming ages he might show the incomparable riches of his grace, expressed in his kindness to us in Christ Jesus" (Ephesians 2:6–7).

THE IMPACT OF A STRONG MARRIAGE

Why is all of this important? Is it so that we can enjoy happy marriages, wonderful families, and terrific anniversary weekend retreats? No! In chapter 4, I pointed out that in Titus 2 the concern for strong marriages was that "no one will malign the word of God." Here, in 1 Peter, the issue is again on a higher plane than just our personal well-being. It is "so that nothing will hinder your prayers" (1 Peter 3:7).

This counters the current tendency to so focus on marriage and family that they nearly become idols to us. Our domestic relationships have a profound impact on our spiritual fellowship. An improper marriage relationship closes the windows of heaven. Our relationship with God our Father can never be right as long as our relationships with His children (especially those closest to us) are wrong.

Notice the assumption that husbands and wives ought to become prayer partners. For all the value of men's and women's prayer groups, they cannot replace the best prayer partner relationship a person can ever have. It is troubling when husbands and wives don't pray together. They try nearly everything else—reading books, consulting counselors, creating strategies to work through a difficult situation. Yet prayer seems to be the final resort instead of the first option. If they are willing to go to counselors, pastors, and books for solutions, how much better it would be to consult the One who created us, who knows us better than we know ourselves, and who loves us enough to die for us.

Surely the devil's strategies succeed when we concede failure in the home for success in some other arena. What is to befall the next generation as the baby boomers age and the "day-care generation" begins to assume positions of responsibility and influence? As we come to our heavenly Father in prayer we can receive the necessary strength to reverse the recent trends of apathy and failure in our marriages. When we come to the throne of grace, God will put everything into perspective.

The scales will fall from our eyes, and we will see ourselves and our lives as they really are.

We will also see our wives as they really are: heavenly gifts, fashioned and shaped by God's loving hand for our completion and joy, because it is not good that we should be alone. As we come to see them in this light, we will desire to fulfill the roles so wisely intended for us.

When we treat our wives as Christ loves the church, the issue of submission ceases to be a problem. If we're doing all *we* should, our wives will become submissive and loving with all their hearts. We will honor, cherish, and protect them. And through it all, God will be glorified before a sinful and cynical world.

WHEN HUSBANDS BECOME FATHERS

Having recognized in the last chapter the interrelationship between the roles of wife and mother, we must now do the same for the husbands. In talking with men, it becomes clear that one of the greatest challenges they face is juggling all the responsibilities. It is often the most diligent of men who feel the greatest challenge. They are trying to please their bosses and respond to their customers. They are trying to live up to the high standards in fulfilling the role of a biblical husband. They also want to be the spiritual leader in their homes, and therefore recognize their responsibility for their children. In many cases, they are living on a fault line, with a growing fear that the big earthquake may come any time and engulf them all.

This growing sense of responsibility, which seems to reach its height in the middle point of a man's life, is often overwhelming. The recent emphasis on men's movements, and the desire for men to find companionship in one another, speak to this issue. It is, therefore, imperative that, as fathers, we understand what the biblical expectations are. One of the reasons for marital failure is the unfulfilled responsibilities of the man in relationship to parenting, sowing seeds of discontent in the mind of his wife.

Years ago, when Merv Griffin asked the late Lucille Ball to give her opinion as to why families were falling apart, she replied succinctly, "Things are falling apart because Papa's gone. If Papa were here, he would fix it." At the risk of oversimplifying the perplexity of today's social problems, it appears clear that the absence of fathers is a key ingredient in the impalpable recipe of teenage suicide, drug abuse, violence, and illegitimacy. Many of us men have become so committed to the art of delegation that we have become skillful in passing off to others what is clearly our responsibility. We expect our wives or church youth group leaders or

Sunday school teachers or baseball counselors or soccer camp coaches to take on the task of nurturing and caring for our kids, while we get on with the "bigger" task of providing the financial resources necessary for those events.

When Paul addresses the fathers as the heads of families in Ephesians 6:4, he points out that the chief responsibility for the training and instruction of the children falls to them. Despite this clear biblical directive, it is still true that regular and meaningful contact between children and their fathers is minimal in far too many cases. Every so often, when a father stands up and takes the reins within his home, people pay attention. One such father was recognized by the syndicated columnist Ann Landers, who carried a letter in her column written by the father to his son, which went as follows:

> Dear Son: As long as you live under this roof you will follow the rules. In our house we do not have a democracy. I did not campaign to be your father. You did not vote for me. We are father and son by the grace of God. I consider it a privilege and I accept the responsibility. In accepting it, I have an obligation to perform the role of a father. I am not your pal. The age difference makes such a relationship impossible. We can share many things, but you must remember that I am your father. This is 100 times more mean-

ingful than being a pal. You will do as I say as long as you live in this house. You are not to disobey me because whatever I ask you to do is motivated by love. This may be hard for you to understand at times, but the rule holds. You will understand perfectly when you have a son of your own. Until then, trust me.

Love, Dad.

This father has the mixture right and his attitude sure. He recognizes his responsibilities and carries them out lovingly and firmly. He isn't far from the picture the New Testament paints of the father as a self-controlled and patient guide and instructor to his children. Such an attitude was a striking contrast to the norm of first-century Greek and Roman culture. The Roman father was an autocrat with the power entrusted and assured by law to sell his children as slaves, chain them to work in the fields, punish them as he determined, and even inflict the death penalty on them.

DO NOT EXASPERATE YOUR CHILDREN

This difference is highlighted in the express injunction Paul gives in Ephesians 6:4: "Fathers, do not exasperate your children." We are not to treat our children in such a way as to embitter or provoke them. While few of us set out with the express purpose of annoying our children, the greater danger is that we may do so unwittingly. It is, therefore, important that we identify the factors that will exasperate our children, causing them to rebel openly or to smolder internally. (Incidentally, even when we do the right things we will often encounter an exasperated child. We need to learn how to discriminate between the expression of legitimate grievance and the expression of rebellion.) Somewhere over the years I've gained a list of nine cautionary recommendations that I think are rich in wisdom.

1. By failing to allow them to be what they are—children.

This is displayed when we make irritating or unreasonable demands that fail to take into account their inexperience and immaturity. It was a wonderful day, not only for Sue and me but also for our son, when we learned, with the help of Dr. James Dobson, to distinguish between willful disobedience and childhood irresponsibility. When we chide our children because they say silly things and are generally silly, instead of being intellectual and mature, then we have probably forgotten that they are children. (This is not to excuse genuinely bad behavior, of course.)

2. By treating them harshly and cruelly.

Our children's lives are fragile. It is important that we don't push our weight around. We may not be guilty of doing this in a physical way, but we may be guilty of verbal brutality. Although most of us have grown up declaring, "Sticks and stones may break my bones, but names will never hurt me," the fact remains that long after the bumps and bruises of life have faded, harmful words may still be imbedded in our children's minds. I can still recall the schoolteacher who used to make children stand up and declare before the class that they had a turnip on their neck, instead of a head. We all laughed uproariously and paid scant attention to the pain that this punishment was inflicting on those tender minds.

Fathers who live in the rough and tumble of a man's world need constantly to remind themselves of the danger of treating their children harshly and unsympathetically.

3. By making fun of them in front of other people, especially their peers.

This often happens unwittingly, and yet it does happen. A father who had hoped to have a boy who was a star athlete but ended up with a son who was a philatelist and computer whiz may be tempted to undermine the qualities of that child in front of others who represent the ideal for which he was looking. The wife is often the more sensitized to this, and she will be able to guard and guide her husband if he has learned to pay attention to the wise and godly counsels of his spouse.

4. By displaying favoritism and comparing one child unfavorably with another.

"Why can't you be like Kevin and get A's all the time?" Even though we may think of this as a means of motivating our children, it is often a source of great discouragement to them. Learning to value each of our children for his or her distinct qualities is an essential part of skillful parenting. This demands that fathers spend sufficient time with their children to be able to commend them for the qualities they are beginning to see. This might mean driving some distance to snowboard shops, just to be able to have the opportunity of company in the car. This may mean closing down the malls with our teenage daughters so that we get the chance to observe their interests and listen to their stories. But unless we are prepared to make the commitment to do so, and to balance the time spent with each one, we may do untold damage.

5. By failing to express approval even when their accomplishments are apparently small.

When I was twelve, our soccer team played in the cup final game in our elementary school league. Much of the game is a blur to me, as you might expect after all these years, but I remember a number of things. First, that I was playing on the right wing and managed to run up and down the field a great deal—but without having much contact with the ball. Second, that although we were very enthusiastic about our chances, we were trounced, five goals to one. Third, that my father stayed for the duration of the game, despite the humiliation that accompanied it.

But more than anything else, I remember the fact that he purchased for me a little medal I have to this day. It was engraved by a jeweler and recorded the fact that we were the "runners up in the cup final of 1964." The very fact that he would take the time to provide that memento for me more than compensated for the pain of the loss. It also provided a stirring reminder for me, (to which I need to pay careful attention as a father of three teenage children) of the importance of pronouncing our approval when our children do well. This is not the same as pronouncing approval always on success, but it is in encouraging them when they have given their best to a task, even though the end result may not have been what they, or we, expected.

6. By being arbitrary in the exercise of discipline.

When we blow hot and cold about discipline, we leave our children in a dilemma. They never know where they stand. One day they are allowed to do something; the next day they are not. On one occasion a certain kind of behavior is acceptable; but on another, it is a punishable offense. We need to learn that the way in which God exercises righteousness and judgment needs to be the standard by which we lay down the parameters and rules of our households. Clarity in these matters will go a long way toward avoiding the confusion and chaos seen in so many homes.

7. By neglecting them and making them feel like an intrusion.

Although we have already noted that part of the task of parenting is preparing our children for leaving us, we nevertheless recognize that while we have them, they are a priority for us. It is important that in their early days, and through their developing years, we let them know just how much we value and cherish them by including them in as much as it is right to include them in. The same remains true in their teenage years. As they make that transition into becoming our friends as well as our children, we need to let them know how much we value their involvement with us and that we do not see their time spent with us as an intrusion.

8. By seeking to make them achieve goals that are clearly not theirs, but ours.

We have all witnessed the sad sight and sounds of the man on the sideline screaming at his obviously incompetent son on the football field: a boy who is there largely out of a desire to please his father, but who, if he were allowed to do what he felt passionate about, would be attending the photographic society or writing software programs for Nintendo games. His father has unfulfilled hopes and dreams in his own life and wants now to see them realized in the life of his boy. This is a tragic mistake, which is repeated again and again and does nothing but exasperate our children.

9. By overprotecting them.

It is usually mothers who fall into the trap of mollycoddling their children and not allowing them the opportunity to breathe freely or to express themselves in a way that is necessary for their development. However, fathers can also be guilty of this and must constantly guard against it. There is a fine line between protecting our children from harm and allowing them the freedom they need to discover just how they are going to make their own way in the world. Every father has to work out his own guidelines for his own children, since he knows them best. But we do well to recognize that one day our children will be in an environment where we are no longer present to protect them. Part of our parenting will be found in skillfully creating opportunities for this element of our children's lives to be fostered.

We certainly don't want our children to grow up diffident and discouraged, so we need to pay careful attention to this word of caution: The development of personality and the blossoming of their gifts will take place within the context of our loving parental encouragement. That's why it is important for us to find good role models in other older men who have been successful in nurturing and caring for their children. We need to be humble enough to ask them just how they did it and what they avoided—and then seek to apply those same principles as we raise our own children.

BUT BRING THEM UP
WISELY AND TENDERLY

Paul not only tells the Ephesians what they are *not* to do, but he also tells them what they *are* to do: "Instead, bring them up in the training and instruction of the Lord" (6:4). In the Greek, Paul uses an interesting and important word for the activity of the father, which is translated in our English versions as "bring them up." It essentially means to nourish or feed them; to cherish them fondly; to rear them tenderly; to sustain them spiritually. We are to enforce for our children and communicate to them the things we believe to be of vital importance. Our children are fragile creatures, and they need the tenderness and the security of our love as we bring them up.

This is a primary responsibility. Of what value will it be that we manage to bring our golf handicap down to single figures in the course of our children's growing up if at the same time we lose the opportunity to build the kind of relationships that will last a lifetime! What if our dogs are champions at the shows, or our flowers win awards in local competitions, if the most precious possessions we've been given by God, namely, our children, are not flourishing and being successful in their lives?

When we think along these lines, we realize that the idea of instantly becoming an effective father is a myth. Parenting takes time. It recognizes failure and disappointment on our part. One of the ways we will build strength into the lives of children is to be vulnerable enough to admit our own weaknesses. Our children not only need to see when we are successful, but need to see that when we fail, we admit it freely. That when we hurt others, we ask for their forgiveness. And that when we've made bad decisions, we seek to correct them quickly.

TRAINING OUR CHILDREN

In other words, we are in training ourselves, and, as we make progress, so in turn we are able to train our children. Hebrews 12:11 says, "No discipline seems pleasant at the time, but painful. Later on, however, it produces a harvest of righteousness and peace for those who have been trained by it." The training to which this refers takes place by means of rules and regulations, rewards, and, when necessary, punishments.

Proverbs 13:24 says, "He who spares the rod hates his son, but he who loves him is careful to discipline him." Proverbs 22:15 says, "Folly is bound up in the heart of a child, but the rod of discipline will drive it far from him." The tendency is for us to become extremists in these things. Either we use excessively stern discipline, or we exercise none at all. In the exercise of punishment, we should be careful *not* to do so when annoyed, or when our pride has been injured. And certainly not when we've lost our temper. If and when we fail in this, we need to be honest enough to admit it to our children and ask for their forgiveness.

In much of the literature today, discipline is described as being simply "corrective," but not "punitive." In actual fact, both elements are involved. We must let our children know that wrongdoing is to be punished and that punishment can be purposeful, provided they respond to it with a correct attitude.

If I read the signs correctly, the great danger in our time is not overbearing parents who exercise discipline too much, but is instead a sorry absence of discipline. In too many cases, fathers are trying to win the approval of their children rather than exercise their rightful parental jurisdiction over them. Writing in an earlier generation, E. K. Simpson says:

> Too many parents now a days, foster the latent mischief of their children by a policy of laisse faire, pampering their pert urchins like pet monkeys whose escapades furnish a fund of amusement as irresponsible freaks of no serious import. Such unbridled young scamps for lack of correction, develop too often into headstrong peevish, self-seeking characters, menaces to the community where they dwell, and the blame rests with their weak-willed and duty-shirking seniors.

We should not allow the quaintness of the language to prevent us from taking the point.

INSTRUCTING OUR CHILDREN

If "training" refers to what we *do* to our children, then "instruction" refers to what we *say* to them. It is very important that we are directive in the way in which we deal with our kids. The contemporary "nondirective" approach of just letting them choose for themselves is to be guarded against at all costs.

The foolishness of this approach was amply expressed in an encounter between the revolutionary Thorwell and the writer Coleridge. Thorwell told Coleridge that he thought it very unfair to give a child's mind a certain bent before it could choose for itself. "I showed him my garden," said Coleridge, "covered with weeds, describing it as a botanical garden." "How so?" he asked. "I replied that it had not yet come to years of discretion. True, the weeds had taken the mean advantage of growing everywhere; but I could not be so unfair as to prejudice the soil in favor of roses and strawberries!"

While guarding against being so directive and domineering that we prevent our children from being able to make decisions and mature, we must teach Christian values of truth and goodness and then defend those values and recommend their acceptance. If this is regarded as indoctrination, then let it be so. It is, in fact, simply to do what the Bible calls us to do—and to take seriously the wonderful privilege of guiding our children and steering them in the direction of righteousness and truth.

We must do this in such a way as to allow our

children to see that behind us stands the Lord Himself, who is the chief teacher and administrator of discipline. Our overriding concern ought to be to bring the heart of our children to the heart of our Savior.

In contrast to all of this, we have this quote, which appeared some time ago, courtesy of the Houston police department: "How to Ruin Your Children: Guaranteed to Be 99 Percent Effective." In part, this is what the leaflet said:

1. Begin with infancy to give the child everything he wants.
2. When he picks up bad words, laugh at him.
3. Never give him any spiritual training. Let him wait until he's twenty-one and then let him decide for himself.
4. Avoid using the word *wrong*. It may develop a serious guilt complex.
5. Pick up everything he leaves lying around so he will be experienced in throwing responsibility on everybody else.[1]

If we are to support our wives in their daily responsibilities of establishing the framework within the home, then we must be seen to be working in partnership with them in the laying down of the guidelines for family life. This demands that we take our responsibilities seriously. Some time ago, I came across a statement of fatherhood that I noted for my own direction and encouragement. I share it here to the same end.

A fact sheet for every father:

1. *I am a dad.* Even on the mornings when I don't feel like it, even when I know I blew it, even when I think I'd rather be doing something else—the central fact of my existence is that I am a husband and a father. There are responsibilities, joys, and sorrows that come with the territory.

2. *The home is the single most important influence on my family.* I can delegate a lot of my responsibilities at work, but I cannot delegate my hopes for my family. The primary values, attitudes, skills, and competencies that my children will grow up with will be learned (or not learned) in my home.

3. *Because of its inherent difficulty and importance, fathering is the most dignified role I will ever play.* Over the years, the dignity of fathering has been eroded. Television has portrayed fathers as buffoons, absentee workaholics, or permissive nice guys who don't have a significant value or ethic in their

heads. It is no wonder that many men have ceased to devote the kind of time and energy the task of real fathering demands.

4. *Being a parent is one of the greatest sources of joy we can ever know.* I really believe that—Murphy's law notwithstanding. There are the impossible moments, but there are also those moments when fathering is just plain fun.

5. *We can all improve.* There are some basic and vital ingredients to good parents which are essential. We can learn what these are and use them. Parenting is not some esoteric art form that can be understood by only a few. With effort, we can all become much better.

6. *Everyone is unique.* Our children are unique and so are we. As we continue to learn from each other, we must accept our uniqueness and discover creative ways to understand and respect one another.

7. *It is difficult to be a good parent.* There are no magic potions or formulas. One of the great myths in our society is that we can be parents without real investment of time and energy. The great truth is that there is no substitute for investment of time and effort. If we accept this truth, we are free

to transcend the problem. Once we have genuinely realized that being a quality father or mother is difficult, then the problem no longer matters. We can get on with what we have to do.[2]

Which of us can evade the challenge that is before us now? A generation of young people is growing up, many of them without the influence of fathers in their homes, let alone godly fathers. It is imperative that we take seriously our responsibilities in this regard. Along with each of you, I face this challenge on a daily basis. I have been greatly convicted by the words of Chuck Swindoll. He is further along in the process, but I can identify with his sentiment when he says, "I'd much rather my brood remember me as the dad who tossed their mother fully clothed into the swimming pool—and lived to tell the story—than the preacher who frowned too much, yelled too loud, talked too long . . . and died too young."[3]

CHAPTER SIX

PULLING WEEDS

To plant a garden is to have weeds. That's the way it goes. They appear overnight, staring up defiantly and threatening to take over the flower bed we have so carefully planted. In our zeal to see them removed, we must exercise care lest we disturb the plants we are trying to cultivate.

My wife is always very wary when I begin one of my manic onslaughts on the weeds, for ignorance coupled with frustration and haste can produce quite a mess. She is usually at hand to point out, "Honey that's an herb, not a weed!"

However, even with these necessary cautions, I know of only one way to deal with weeds: immediately, ruthlessly, and consistently. As in our garden, so too in our marriages. Not all weeds are ugly. In fact, sometimes they make an attractive addition to the plant life. But we cannot be seduced by their attraction. They must come out or we will regret it. Neglect will find our gardens overgrown in no time at all, and in need of a major work project, usually involving outside help. There are obviously various weeds and we cannot list them all, but let's identify some of the most common.

UNBROKEN TIES TO THE PAST

Prior to marriage, we all have a number of loyalties and dependencies. But as soon as we take that wedding vow, our primary human relationship becomes our spouse. This brand-new relationship forever alters previous associations, even of the best sort.

Problems emerge whenever individuals do not sever emotional ties to old boyfriends or girlfriends. This is especially true when there has been a heavy physical component in a prior relationship. The bonding that took place was premature and wrong. Unless the individual works hard with God's help to stop reliving the old dreams and schemes of the past, then both the person and his or her spouse will suffer.

I am not suggesting that a person won't experience a sudden unexpected recollection that comes from nowhere to wound like a fiery dart. We can, however, stop *pursuing* the emotional memory of a previous love. We must root out those recollections from our memories to the best of our abilities. When all we do is chop the heads off weeds, then all we enjoy is temporary relief from their presence. They will be back—often in a more robust form than before.

I have seen the destructive weed of past ties wrap itself so tightly around a husband or wife that divorce is the result. In many such cases, the individual then seeks out and marries his or her previous lover. At the heart of these matters is a theological issue—the difference between remorse and genuine repentance. A person may think he has repented of the sins of his past and moved on with his life, when actually he's just very sorry that things didn't work out.

If you need help determining the difference, you can be sure that repentance hates the memory of sin and resists its return at every point. But if the sorrow you feel keeps you focused on the past, beware of remorse that may be preventing you from acknowledging the root of sin. If you do not find a previous sinful relationship unattractive, you must get beyond the remorse to find the repentance you need.

If the husband and/or wife has been divorced, this problem is inevitably compounded, for the aftereffects of divorce are often more severe than the divorce itself. As the couple approaches marriage, one (or both) of them faces especially strong ties to the past that almost certainly will work their way into this brand-new relationship.

Let's assume that Bill and Jane, both divorced, are planning to marry. Neither of them initiated their divorces, and, in fact, did all they could to save their marriages. Bill's wife left him for a fitness trainer at their club. Jane's husband came home one evening and announced that he was strongly attracted to his secretary and wanted to be "amicably" released from his marriage. What can Bill and Jane expect in their new relationship?

Sin causes misery. Even though Bill and Jane could do little to avoid their divorces, they and their children are forced to live with the consequences of their former spouses' sin. From now on, there will be occasional friction with the children of the previous marriage, who are forced to commute between divorced parents. When the children graduate or get married, those events will become major stress points as Bill and Jane attempt to celebrate with their kids in the shadow of new stepparents. If Bill and Jane have children of their own, there will be a natural rivalry between those children and the children of the ex-spouses. Whether or not Bill and Jane choose to dwell on the ties of the past, those once vital relationships will assert themselves at regular occasions.

Couples do not need to feel trapped by these old associations, but moving on with their lives will require an extraordinary measure of emotional fortitude and prayerful dependence on God. It will also be a great help if they cultivate the kind of sensitive openness that will allow them to acknowledge their emotional struggles to each other. With honesty and patience, they can lean on each other, and together rest in the promise of God's provision and protection.

It is really a bit of an old chestnut, but when it comes to the issue of unbroken ties, we must also recognize the "in-law factor." The underlying factor in establishing a proper postmarital relationship with both parents and in-laws is in learning to prayerfully and sensibly submit to the Scripture that says: "For this reason a man will leave his father and mother and be united to his wife, and they will become one flesh" (Genesis 2:24).

As grateful as a man may be for the guidance and help he has received from his parents, it is imperative for the well-being of all concerned that he understands the importance of heading up a whole new separate decision-making unit. In the same way, the wife must play her part in disallowing her parents from making undue demands on her time and affection, since she is now under the headship of her husband.

It is not that in-laws deliberately set out to cause problems. In most cases, they would be mortified to think that their actions were viewed in that way, but unless care is taken to ensure that there is a clean break—emotionally and financially and in every other way—then untold harm may well be the result. In *The Other Woman in Your Marriage,* Norman Wright quotes a fine illustration of cutting the apron strings.

> I'll never forget the wedding of one of my best college friends, John Engstrom, years ago. Actually it wasn't the wedding itself that impressed me as much as something that happened at the rehearsal dinner. Mrs. Engstrom, John's mum, was seated at the front table with John, his bride, and the bride's parents. At a particular time at the dinner, Mrs. Engstrom stood up and pulled out a beautifully wrapped box. She unwrapped it, and with great ceremony displayed one of her favorite old aprons. Holding the apron high for everyone to see, she reached into her purse and brought out a big pair of scissors. With a flourish, she snipped off the apron strings and handed them to John's bride-to-be.
>
> "Never again," she said, "will I have the same place in John Engstrom's life. You are now the woman in his life."
>
> It was a moment of formal releasing, in front of

many witnesses. And the most significant witnesses of all were a young bride and groom. It was a profound moment . . . but a joyful one, too. There was a feeling of rightness about it all.[1]

KID STUFF

"Sons are a heritage from the Lord, children a reward from him" (Psalm 127:3). Given all that the Scriptures have to say about children, we surely cannot be suggesting that we should perceive them as part of our weeding project. Well, no. Obviously not the children themselves, but there are certain aspects related to children that have to be dealt with if we are to avoid marital disruption and even failure.

A LACK OF DESIRE TO HAVE CHILDREN

The first factor may strike us as strange initially. I am referring to certain couples who declare that they have no interest in becoming parents at all, ever. Where there are peculiar circumstances of age or illness that may be even unknown to the general public, then we should have nothing to say. But when this nonparenting posture is driven either by fear or, even worse, by selfishness, then I believe that the couple is in need of help. There may well be underlying factors of which they themselves are not even aware and which, if left unattended, will manifest themselves in other ways that are likely to be destructive. Certainly the expectation of Scripture is that married couples would gladly anticipate the gift of children. Since the Scriptures are silent on such specifics, we must be on our guard against an undue dogmatism that will be harmful to some. We do well to heed the warning to judge nothing before the appointed time.

THE INABILITY TO HAVE CHILDREN

The second factor is the reverse of the first, namely, couples who are facing stress in their marriages because they are apparently unable to have children. I am told that one out of every six women in America is infertile. It is not uncommon to listen to couples berate themselves for their past and sometimes even blame each other for the absence of children. Since God alone is the author of life, they need to come to the place of resolute trust in His providence. It is possible that He has plans for them that will in retrospect allow them to see their childlessness as a blessing and not, as they are tempted to think now, a judgment. For others, it is God's perfect plan in the adoption of little ones for whom they would never have cause to care if they had become parents in the natural order of things.

At the same time, we cannot underestimate the influence for good that childless couples have had as extended members of families as well as in unique ministries that demand time and effort which they could never have given if they were fulfilling the role of parents. When our children first came along, we benefited greatly from the kindness and love shown to us by an older couple two doors away who, although they never had children, were perfectly suited to the role of aunt and uncle. Our children's photographs held pride of place within their home and the joy they experienced was second only to the help we received.

We need to be especially aware of the woman for whom all this parenting, adopting, and mothering business has just never come out right. She has the potential to channel her energies for great good but if she fails to do so, then she will often be a very unhappy and cantankerous person. One meets this rarely in pastoral ministry, but when encountered it requires peculiar wisdom and grace both to address honestly and then to give guidance graciously.

SHORTSIGHTEDNESS IN PLANNING FAMILIES

Another problem can emerge for couples with no apparent plan for an ever-growing family. Regardless of one's views on contraception, most people agree that parents should make adequate provisions for the emotional, spiritual, social, financial, and educational needs of their children.

Some couples use sanctimonious language to hide the fact that they are being irresponsible in this area. There is little doubt that many of them should be placing the emphasis of their parenting skills on quality rather than quantity. Again, each couple must do as they see fit, yet many marital struggles are at least partially self-induced by the absence of prayerful planning for offspring.

I rejoice when I see wonderful examples of extra-large, happy, well-functioning families. Unfortunately, these seem to be the exception rather than the norm.

WHEN CHILDREN PLAY PARENTS AGAINST EACH OTHER

The discipline of children is frequently a major point of contention between parents. Many times husbands leave all discipline matters to their wives, who almost always become frustrated by their husbands' lack of support.

It is crucial for husbands and wives to agree on a strategy of discipline, beginning when their children are toddlers and continuing through their teenage years. Otherwise, the family risks becoming another tragically divided home where children are barriers between husband and wife rather than expressions of their parents' harmony of heart, mind, and purpose.

Suppose, for example, the wife has been led to believe that spanking is tantamount to child abuse. The husband, on the other hand, is quick to quote Proverbs 22:15: "Folly is bound up in the heart of a child, but the rod of discipline will drive it far from him." This couple is going to need help in coming to agreement on a unified approach to discipline. It becomes for the wife an issue of submission, first to the Scriptures and then to her husband. For the husband, it becomes a pressing, challenging opportunity to exercise his role of sacrificial leadership!

Coming to an agreement is not always easy, but it must be done for the sake not only of the children, but of the marriage.

WHEN CHILDREN SEEM TO BE ALL THAT HOLDS THE MARRIAGE TOGETHER

This problem is the opposite extreme of the previous one. In this case, instead of the children dividing Mom and Dad, they are used as a glue to try to keep a shaky marriage intact.

This problem is not easy to detect until it has already become an established pattern. Sometimes it only becomes apparent when the children leave home. Still, there are clear signs along the way. For example, when the kids are all away at Grandpa's house for the weekend and conversation between husband and wife is stilted and empty, the writing should be on the wall. Perhaps only then do the parents realize that their only animated communication takes place when the focus is the children.

It is important to remember that in the divine order of things, the kids are intended to leave while the parents remain at home. In the process of family life, parents have a dual responsibility. First, they are supposed to prepare their children by helping them develop a sense of healthy independence before sending them out into the world. But second, and just as important, parents are supposed to prepare themselves for a lifetime together by strengthening the marriage bond and improving communication between themselves. If daily communication involves little more than a series of questions and answers related to the children's school schedules, the parents have a long way to go in their own interpersonal development.

STOP THE MERRY-GO-ROUND

Another area of potential difficulty relates to the frenetic pace parents set for their children or are influenced by their children to set. In an attempt to produce "well-rounded" kids, we are in danger of simply going round in circles. Tennis, music lessons, ballet, and tai-kwon-do—and that was only Saturday's schedule!

In this we risk giving the child the impression that life is an amusement park and Mom and Dad the tour guides. By the time the guides have packed the train and remembered their uniforms, they find that they have little left to give to each other. Beware the marital malaise that can subtly begin in such a scenario.

We sometimes say that our children "grow like weeds." But in all these matters, you can see how children might also *act* as weeds in your marriage garden. A wrong kind of preoccupation regarding their presence or absence or discipline can intensify the stress of a marriage if the problems aren't dealt with quickly and completely.

TAKING EACH OTHER FOR GRANTED

I was the guest of a family in Australia, and we had just finished our meal. In the absence of a dishwasher (a mechanical one, that is), I volunteered to help with the task. In declining my offer, the young wife assured me that it would be taken care of by her husband, Lionel. Then she turned and said, "Oh, Lionel loves doing the dishes, don't you, Lionel?"

Neither she nor I was prepared for Lionel's response and the underlying sense of bitterness that accompanied it: "No, I *don't* enjoy doing the dishes." He then made clear that the reason he had been doing the dishes ever since they had been married (some twelve years) was because of his frustration with the way his wife cleaned the house. Her assumption had been all wrong, and Lionel had never discussed the matter with her in a constructive manner. After I poked my unfortunate nose into this hornet's nest, I spent the remainder of my stay trying to help this young couple pull some large weeds from their marital garden.

Not every situation is as serious as this one, but each couple must learn to eliminate the selfishness that is often at the root of taking one another for granted. Husbands are called to live in *consideration* of their wives. They must ensure that the passing of time and familiarity with routine does not deaden their sense of wonder and awe for the immense privilege of waking up each morning next to this woman who is an express gift of God for life. It is all too easy to neglect to provide genuine expressions of gratitude because we have come to believe that our spouse is just doing what is expected and it is not deserving of special mention.

We can check how well we are doing in this area by listening to ourselves talk. How often do we use the words *thank you,* or *I appreciate you,* or *I can't do without you?* We can ask ourselves how long it has been since we complimented our spouse for some aspect of their character or their appearance. We might check to see when we last spent a special card or flowers or came home early so that they could have some time of their own free from other responsibilities.

It is too bad that we assume that intermittent bursts of appreciation, often driven by guilt, will be sufficient to compensate for the lack of consideration on a daily basis. It is not so much in the big events that we express this, although we do not want to miss the opportunities created by birthdays and anniversaries, but it is in the casual routine of apparently inconsequential events that we make it clear that we are not taking them for granted. In the sixties, someone sang about the fact that it was "those little things that you do that make me glad I'm in love with you. The way you walk, the way you hold my hand, the way you talk and make me understand—you know I love those *little things that you do!*"

I came across a wonderful example some time ago. It was a note written by a wife to her husband:

Dear Wally,
  I want to say "thank you" for a wonderful time away. The beauty of the mountains and the golf courses were superb. The time with you was wonder-

ful. You are my beloved husband, as well as a fun companion and friend. Thank you for the beautiful little box with stationery in it. This is a sheet from it —love the dainty design of it and the pretty color. The Lord gave me the very best when He gave me you. I love you more now than the day we married.

All my love,
Dolores

What I found most stirring about this letter was not the content, but the context. This wasn't a note from a young woman in the early blush of marital excitement. It was written by a woman in her seventies, who had been married to Wally for forty-nine years! Judging by this example, I would guess that, in the course of those forty-nine years, Wally and Dolores had written enough notes to each other to wallpaper their house!

If you find that you have been ignoring a taking-my-spouse-for-granted weed, pull it up right now and fill the gaping hole with flowers of appreciation or thoughtful words of gratitude. If you are stuck for words, close your eyes and imagine what you would have said in your courting days. Digging deep into that well will bring up sweet water.

THE COMPARISON TRAP

Over dinner, a wife tells her husband, "I was over having coffee with Jean today, and she said her husband is teaching the men's Bible study, memorizing all of Second Timothy, and considering an evening class at the local seminary." If you were the husband, wouldn't you fill in the inferred, unspoken conclusion: "Why can't you be more like him?"

The husband was well aware of his need to grow spiritually. In fact, as he had been driving home that very evening he had congratulated himself for maintaining a steady Bible reading program during the past month. That was the first time he had been so consistent. But his joy instantly evaporated as a result of his wife's unhelpful comparison.

Or consider the reverse situation, where a husband regularly goads his wife with such comments as: "Are you ever going to read a book all the way through? And when you do, will it be something other than one of those cheap romance novels?" The husband's questions bite deep into his wife's psyche. She knows he feels superior. Ever since he joined the neighborhood reading group, he has used what he was learning there, not as a basis for meaningful conversation, but instead as a way of comparing her unfavorably with other local wives who enjoy opinionated discussion. She is bright and intelligent, but she views the book discussions as stodgy. She has numerous other outlets for her interests and intelligence, but the unfavorable comparisons still hurt.

Even more common are the critical comments regarding physical characteristics. "I saw Jerry down at the courts. Now there's someone who has managed to keep a waistline!" Instinctively the husband sucks in his stomach and regrets the gradual increase of his belt size. It may even be worse when the wife is on the receiving end of a husband's comparison. Some insensitive men use anorexic waiflike supermodels as a standard by which they compare all other women. A much better strategy is found in the wisdom of Solomon:

> May you rejoice in the wife of your youth. A loving doe, a graceful deer—may her breasts satisfy you always, may you ever be captivated by her love. Why be captivated, my son, by an adulteress? Why embrace the bosom of another man's wife? (Proverbs 5:18–20)

Solomon's challenge is to rejoice in the wife *of your youth,* not a wife *who looks like a youth.* Faithfulness across years brings a deepening sense of love and appreciation, but engaging in mental comparisons introduces seeds of disintegration.

I recently received a letter from a radio listener which illustrates this point:

Dear Mr. Begg,

While listening to your reference to Solomon's instruction to enjoy "the wife of one's youth," I remembered an incident which I thought you might like. The night my husband and I met, I wore the kind of skin-tight bright purple jumpsuit which only looks good on someone as young and slender as I was then.

Shortly after giving birth to our eldest daughter, I felt enormous, old, and depressed. Tearfully I told my husband: "Inside I'm still the girl in the purple jumpsuit, but outside I feel like a whale!" My husband launched a secret mission to buy me a new purple jumpsuit. (I'd given the old one to the Salvation Army in a fit of closet cleaning.) As purple jumpsuits were not exactly in season that year, he had to go to seven different stores, explaining persistently to each puzzled clerk that yes, it HAD to be a jumpsuit, and yes, it HAD to be purple. Finally he found one (one size fits all), and presented it to me with a card I cherish: "Sweetheart, you'll always be the girl in the purple jumpsuit to me."

This kind of love and encouragement can only come about when we resist the temptation to compare our spouses unfavorably with others in terms of body, mind, and spirit. Such comparisons are weeds that can strangle even the best of relationships.

RUMMAGING AROUND IN THE PAST

It is imperative that we determine not to dig up old failures or past disappointments. It's not pleasant to be reminded of things that have been forgiven and should have been long forgotten. While couples may enjoy going through old possessions at a rummage sale, going back through old points of contention should be avoided at all costs.

The best fertilizer for this particular weed is any current disagreement. Perhaps the husband is stung by his wife's truthful and justifiable admonition. If he is unwilling to admit the truth of what she says, and is at a loss for a response, the temptation may arise to dredge up something *she* has done wrong in the past. He introduces today what should have been left alone as part of yesterday. How ironic that the same man who can't remember where he left his car keys five minutes ago has the capacity to remember offenses from five years ago!

One of the strategies of the evil one is to convince us to rummage around in the garbage cans of forgiven sin. Therefore, we must learn to live in openness with our spouses. We should be slow to take offense and quick to grant forgiveness. Paul's words to the Ephesian believers are applicable here: "Be kind and compassionate to one another, forgiving each other, just as in Christ God forgave you" (Ephesians 4:32).

Unless a couple learns to keep short accounts

of offenses, the residue of resentment builds until it eventually hardens the arteries of their love, severely impairing the marriage. The past must be put well behind them if they are to face the future without fear and enjoy the present unashamed. As Jay Adams expresses it: "Nothing new and bright can be built for the future until the rubble of the past is cleared away."[2]

This raises the perennial question about whether a spouse guilty of an extramarital affair should inform his or her spouse. Pastors and counselors disagree on this matter. It is an area calling for extreme sensitivity and caution, and many considerations must be taken into account. In the majority of cases where the affair is not confessed, the guilty party senses the other spouse suspects something is wrong. When there is no confession, deception and deceit become barriers to the truthful transparency that allows intimacy at every level.

On the other hand, the offending party must also consider the emotional health of the spouse and the potential impact on the children. Therefore, the context of disclosure should take into account three things: timing, place, and personnel.

In seeking to help couples in this area I have observed that it is never easy to confess marital infidelity to a spouse. Few things are as stressful as being suddenly confronted with the news that one's husband or wife has been unfaithful. Handling the shock of this realization will take essentially all the emotional stamina one can muster. For example, let's say a husband wants to confess an affair to his wife. If she is dealing with the impending death of a parent or is about to be hospitalized for surgery, then wisdom would suggest waiting for a more appropriate occasion. The harsh truth of the announcement is bad enough; the timing need not make it worse.

The matter of *where* to make the announcement may seem insignificant, but I would suggest choosing a neutral location. Some places are associated with joyful occasions of the past, and they need not be marred by this news. Other locations will be commonplace to both spouses in the future, and it is not wise to connect them with such negative memories. It is far better to give a little thought to identifying a remote place to share the news that isn't likely to be a regular source of pain in the days to come.

What I mean by *personnel* is a third party to act as an emotional bridge or buffer when the confession is made. This is a situation where one person is well aware of what is about to be said, but the other is completely in the dark. An impartial third party can help mediate—holding the guilty person accountable while trying to minimize hostile and/or critical comments from the injured person.

No clear biblical mandate is provided for how to handle this delicate situation, so it is the personal decision of the party involved. However, I like what Norman Wright suggests:

> Even though each person involved in an affair must make up his own mind, to me it seems best to confess it to God and to one's spouse, realizing that there is no guarantee of acceptance, forgiveness, or restoration from the offended spouse. (But God always forgives and forgets.) If the affair is not confessed, and if it is discovered in the years to come, the effect could be even more upsetting. The one involved could spend years in fear that the discovery may occur, whereas the individual may have to live with his mate's wrath and suspicion for only a matter of weeks or months after the confession.[3]

To my surprise, I found the same advice being offered in a recent issue of *Men's Health* magazine. This quote is from Frank Pittman III, the author of *Private Lies: Infidelity and the Betrayal of Intimacy:*

> If you love your wife, truly regret your error and absolutely want to keep your marriage healthy and intact, the only thing to do is confess. That's right,

own up. Why? It's the only way to have a real marriage. As long as you're carrying this baggage around, you can never get close to your wife again. Keep that one moment of weakness secret and your marriage will have termites for years to come. If you don't openly acknowledge it, you'll only make it easier to do it again. Ask yourself what kind of guy you want to be. Do you want to be that kind of guy? If not, "fess up."[4]

Some spouses have genuine concerns: What if the offended party decides to end the relationship and pursue divorce? What if he or she continues to burn with anger and resentment, refusing to forgive and forget?

Most people need a deeper understanding of what genuine forgiveness involves. Forgiveness does not mean "looking the other way" and ignoring the fact that the event ever took place. Nor is it an emotional surge that eradicates the matter from recollection once and for all. Instead, true forgiveness is an act of the will. By God's grace, one person determines not to allow the painful memory of another person's past offense to become our companion in the present. As time goes by, the offended person learns to say no to self-pity and anger, and yes to forgiveness and reconciliation. The process of forgiveness takes time, but as we forge ahead, we look to One who is able to do infinitely more than we ever dare to ask or imagine.

Another consideration is whether confession of sin is to be public or private. John Stott points out some of the biblical principles in his book *Confess Your Sins:*

Some zealous believers, in their anxiety to be open and honest, go too far in this matter. To say, "I'm sorry I was rude to you," or, "I'm sorry I showed off in front of you," is right; but not, "I'm afraid I've had jealous thoughts about you all day." Such a confession does not help; it only embarrasses. If the sin remains secret in the mind and does not erupt into words or deeds, it must be confessed to God alone. It is true that, according to the teaching of Jesus, "anyone who looks at a woman lustfully has already committed adultery with her in his heart." But this is adultery in the sight of God and is to be confessed to Him, not to her. The rule is always that secret sins must be confessed secretly (to God) and private sins must be confessed privately (to the injured party). Perhaps a word of caution may be written here. All sins, whether of thought, word, or deed must be confessed to God, because He sees them all. "O Lord, you have searched me and you know me. You know when I sit and when I rise; you perceive my thoughts from afar. You discern my going out and my lying down; you are familiar with all my ways. Before a word is on my tongue you know it completely, O Lord" (Psalm 139:1–4). But we need to remember that men do not share the omniscience of God. They hear our words and see our works; they cannot read our hidden thoughts. It is therefore, social sins of word and deed which we must confess to our fellow-men, not the sinful thoughts we may have harbored about them.[5]

When I was an assistant minister, I recall an occasion when an incident took place that had great potential harm for our congregation. In the aftermath, the pastor called upon the people to adopt a motion of forgetfulness and by so doing to pledge themselves never to speak of the details of what took place. The desire was not to squash the truth—the matter had already been dealt with—but it was simply to recognize the potential harm there was in reintroducing a matter which had been banished in the sea of God's forgetfulness. All married couples to one degree or another will have in their history incidents they would do well to bury and determine never to make midnight sojourns to the graveyard to dig up the bones. While it may be true that we cannot forget, we can also choose not to remember.

IGNORING COMMON SENSE BOUNDARIES

If it has not already become an axiom in your marriage, then make it one as of today: *Do not take someone of the opposite sex into precincts that are the exclusive domain of your spouse.* One of the most common "weeds" mentioned in association with marital failure is naïveté in what is shared with members of the opposite sex other than the person's spouse.

When a man tells me he "communicates" far better with the lady in the office than he does with his wife, the danger signals are flashing. It's eye-opening to hear how often an extramarital affair begins with casual conversation around the water cooler, while having coffee together, or in some other "innocent" arena. Yet anytime one person takes a discussion into new levels of intimacy beyond what he or she shares with a spouse, the weed sprouts and begins to bloom.

Sometimes the interest in the other person is perceived as purely spiritual, yet often becomes romantic and eventually moves into a sinful entanglement. When a man tells me that his only interest in a woman is spiritual, I like to ask whether he would be as interested if she weighed another one hundred pounds and had a body-builder husband! If someone is more concerned about the spiritual well-being of a stranger than the strength of his or her own marriage, then something is wrong.

We should certainly be concerned for friends and colleagues to be brought to faith. However, it is better to connect them with a mature Christian of their own gender to prevent any mixing of motives. While this may be regarded as a little extreme, I would rather be on the safe side than risk adding to the sorry statistics of marital disintegration.

The prevalence of women in the workplace has made a direct impact on the number of extramarital affairs. One of my friends, the president and CEO of a large manufacturing company, told me he finally canceled his off-site company conferences. They took place in hotels over a number of days, and he observed that the extent of extramarital "fooling around" was epidemic. He determined not to provide the opportunity for that to take place. He was widely criticized, but held his ground!

Jay Adams has as much experience and wisdom as any in the matter of counseling. He also refers to this problem in his book *Solving Marriage Problems:*

> Job influences are crucial simply because much of one's week is spent with business associates. That prolonged and regular contact may easily lead to dangerously close associations with evil companions. Unless, therefore, one draws clear limits to his associations and resolves not to transgress those limits, he will naturally drift towards companionships that could harm him and his marriage. . . . The businessman, like the preacher, should heed Paul's advice:

"Treat the younger women as sisters" (1 Timothy 5:2). No sounder approach is possible.[6]

Again, the *Men's Health* article by Frank Pittman agrees with the Christian perspective:

> Consider that most virulent of monogamy manglers, the business trip. Safety rule number one: Don't ever be alone in a hotel room with a woman who is not your mom, your sister, or your wife. No exceptions. Don't stop by just to pick up the new sales data or drop off the old sales data. Forget the data, all right? Just don't go there. Period.[7]

WHO SAYS MARRIAGE HAS TO BE THIS WAY?

According to a recent poll, 66 percent of Americans believe that "there is no such thing as absolute truth." Among young adults, the percentage is even higher: 72 percent of those between nineteen and twenty-five do not believe absolutes exist. Even among those who call themselves evangelical Christians, 53 percent expressed a belief that there are no absolutes.[8]

How is it that the same people who assert a belief in the authority of Scripture and the claims of Jesus Christ can deny absolute truth? This very contradiction is an indication of the dilemma we face.

It is difficult to think of a contemporary moral issue that does not reflect a more liberal interpretation today than in years past. Not long ago, the killing of a child in its mother's womb was considered an atrocity; today it is legal and regarded by the majority as acceptable. Twenty years ago, it was considered an unthinkable crime to kill the handicapped, the elderly, and those who had lost the will to live; today it is perceived as an act of compassion. After all, in a world without absolutes, who is to say just what is right or wrong?

Perhaps nowhere has society's thinking changed more drastically than in regard to sex outside of marriage. Once clearly regarded by the majority as wrong, now only about one-third of the population thinks so. And when we come to the matter of marriage itself, anyone who promotes absolute standards and clearly defined roles for men and women must be prepared to face "the slings and arrows of outrageous fortune." But if we are to uphold the Maker's instructions, we have no other alternative open to us.

The ever increasing percentages of failed marriages should indicate that secular society's approach to marriage with its lack of absolutes is not working. A significant number of movies have challenged the institution of marriage under the disguise of humor. For example, *Mr. Mom, Three Men and a Baby, Tootsie, Mrs. Doubtfire,* and, most recently, *The Birdcage,* which deals with the implications of same-sex marriage. It is important now, as in every age, that we learn the times in which we are living; so that we can avoid its temptations and challenge its proud assertions. Many of the things that are accepted as natural—perhaps even beautiful—are nothing more than weeds.

No matter how much effort goes into the preparation and planting of a garden, it will all be in vain if the weeds are not dealt with. Let us then resolve to tackle them immediately, ruthlessly, and consistently.

CHAPTER SEVEN

PLANTING HEDGES

England is a land of hedges. They come in all shapes and sizes. Some are fashioned with care; others grow wild and haphazardly. Hedges serve as a line of demarcation between properties and as a source of protection from the elements. The care with which the average Englishman tends to his hedgerow indicates its importance—it is not simply as a thing of beauty, but is a boundary.

Robert Frost suggested that "good fences make good neighbors." So, too, do good hedges. Interestingly, these leafy fences are not allowed in certain neighborhoods where the preference is to eliminate visible boundary lines between properties. One is immediately tempted to see in this a parable of human relationships. Freedom of movement between places and people may offer great potential, yet can be fraught with danger.

The institution of marriage also needs boundaries and protection. The principles that "hedge in" a healthy marriage are biblical in their substance and practical in their expression.

CAREFULNESS

The principle is found in the words of Paul: "Let the man who feels sure of his standing today be careful that he does not fall tomorrow" (1 Corinthians 10:12, PHILLIPS).

This is not a call for us to live in paralyzing fear. We need not go through each day imagining all the dreadful things that could befall us. That would be like driving from Cleveland to Detroit at 65 mph, continually worrying about a wheel falling off or the engine catching fire. After we make adequate preparations for the journey, we then must proceed carefully, but not in constant fear.

It *is* a call to live realistically, with that healthy measure of skepticism to which we were referring. We need to ensure that we are honest with ourselves when it comes to the temptation we feel to run the red light or park a little longer than is allowed. We need to be vigilant in guarding our spouses from potential encroachments upon the marriage relationship which they may not detect.

If a builder were working around my house and took even a casual interest in my wife, I would consider it a possible forewarning to danger. We live in a fallen world where sin is pervasive. Yet it is important to be skeptical without becoming cynical.

In the course of the past twenty-two years, as I have had the sorry task of listening to couples describe the demise of their marriages, the recurring phraseology includes: "We regarded ourselves as the last people to be facing this." There, it seems to me, is part of the problem. It is foolishness to live in a kind of naïveté that assumes immunity from the external forces that would work against our marriages. It is certainly not wise to allow our minds to be continually exposed to the ungodly thinking of our day in films and songs and books and then to assume that we are somehow miraculously unaffected by it.

At the same time, we are being less than honest if we do not acknowledge the constant downward pull of our own selfish desires and the reality of failing to do the good we planned and sadly doing the bad we were hoping to avoid.

Our approach to marriage should be similar to preparing for a transatlantic flight. Before every trip, the cabin crew goes through the safety instructions, preparing passengers for the worst while expecting the best. We need to be realistic enough to take precautions that will save us from falling into the traps so skillfully set by our adversary. Remember Peter's warning: "Be self-controlled and alert. Your enemy the devil prowls around like a roaring lion looking for someone to devour" (1 Peter 5:8).

ENDEAVOR

We dare not assume that a healthy marriage can be developed and enjoyed without some solid hard work. Perhaps you have witnessed a transformation in a neighbor's yard when a new owner moved in. The dandelion garden of epidemic proportions becomes a plush green lawn. Previously unkempt pathways are now manicured and bordered with flowers. Piles of ivy are trimmed back to reveal small stone walls that define the various flower beds. The herbaceous borders are now tailored with an exquisite eye for detail. What can we deduce from the metamorphosis? Certainly that the new owners love to garden, but more than that, they were also prepared to put in hours of hard work to restore the jungle to an area of order and beauty.

Solomon described the field of a man who lacked judgment: "Thorns had come up everywhere, the ground was covered with weeds, and the stone wall was in ruins" (Proverbs 24:31). As he pondered the sorry sight, he noted that laziness and neglect allow poverty to sneak up on us like a bandit (vv. 32–34).

If we live in a shambles long enough, we may become unaware of how bad things really are. The same is true of a marriage. As I discussed in chapter 6, it's easy to allow weeds to overtake a marriage by just doing nothing! However, if we want a beautiful marriage that is attractive, we will have to approach it with all the care and hard work of a gardener.

It helps for couples to begin with an overall plan that will help them regularly assess where they are and where they are going. Some couples are very disciplined about this. They take time out on a regular basis to reflect on the past and determine where they hope to be in five years. They evaluate the strategic points along the journey: the arrival of children, the development of careers, the college years, the decisions of retirement.

It is important for couples to think through changes together. One person may be more concerned than the other, but both must take time to ensure that they face the future with a united plan of action. During these discussions they learn how to defer to one another.

We also need to have an eye for detail, watching to ensure that we do not allow destructive pests to infest our garden and begin to spread. I recently read a letter from a lady in her sixties who was bothered when her husband opened mail addressed directly to her. This immediately caught my attention because I tend to be guilty of the same thing. It was not, she said, that she wanted to keep anything from her husband. They always read everything to each other anyway. It was simply that she looked forward to the joy of opening her own mail. Her husband was depriving her of this small privilege, oblivious to his wife's desire. Care in little things makes a huge contribution to the enjoyment of the marriage relationship.

As healthy gardens need water, so marriages need the regular watering of God's Word. Unless we make Scripture a daily part of our lives and sit under its instruction, we are in danger of having everything we value dry up around us. God's Word prunes us, allowing us to grow in healthy ways and into beautiful shapes. It helps us identify and eliminate weeds that deprive the relationship of needed nourishment. Selfish neglect, stony silence, and stormy outbursts are just a few other ugly intruders with which we must deal ruthlessly. Only with God's help can we commit to saying no to selfishness and yes to selflessness.

COMMUNICATION

"Before I was married, I would lie awake at night thinking of all that my fiancée had told me that evening. Now that I am married, I fall asleep before my wife has stopped talking!"

This vaguely humorous statement comes too close to the truth for many couples. When tracing the reasons for extramarital affairs, people frequently come to realize that one of the major appeals of the other person had been his or her listening ear. Somewhere along the journey of life together, the couple had stopped listening to each other. Soon after losing the will to listen, many then lose the desire to talk. And without knowing what is going on inside each other's head, a marriage has little chance to survive.

Communication is essential to all human relationships, and it is particularly vital if we are to cultivate the level of intimacy that is God's design for marriage. In preparing for marriage, this issue must be addressed and the potential pitfalls identified. It helps when newlyweds are already friends who have shared their thoughts and opinions on a variety of topics—and desire to know more.

The origin of communication breakdown can be traced to Adam and Eve. Prior to Adam's sin, there had been perfect communication between God and man, and between man and woman. They were naked, there was complete openness between them, and yet they knew no shame. But sin caused them to suddenly start covering their bodies and hiding from God.

That was just the beginning of the cover-up trend. Jay Adams points out how the same problem continues in marriages today:

> Unconfessed and unforgiven sin always leads to a cover-up with its inevitable consequence: a breakdown in one's relationship with others. . . . Husbands hide from their wives, and wives cover up parts of their lives, when there is unresolved sin. In order to reestablish communication in intimacy, it is first necessary to eliminate the sin that is blocking the communication.[1]

"But that's just the way I am," protests the husband, explaining why he doesn't talk to his wife very much. What he *doesn't* come right out and say is, "And don't expect me to change!" Adams suggests that our response to this kind of assertion should be: "Doubtless that is the way you are, but it is not the way God wants you to be, and if you will only confess your sin and do as He says, that is not the way you will be in the future."[2]

When we understand this, we are no longer satisfied to hide behind the excuses of temperament or childhood patterns. The bad news is that change may be difficult and even a bit painful. The good news is that our lives can be *much* better. We don't have to stay forever in the harmful rut we've carved for ourselves.

With God's help, any consistent patterns of poor behavior can be replaced with holy habits and actions. This is the hope which Paul held out to the Ephesian believers. The impact of his words comes out with striking clarity in the Phillips paraphrase:

> This is my instruction, then, which I give you in the Lord's name. Do not live any longer the futile lives of gentiles. For they live in a world of shadows, and are cut off from the life of God through their deliberate ignorance of mind and sheer hardness of herart. They have lost all decent feelings and abandoned themselves to sensuality, practising any form of impurity which lust can suggest. But you have learned nothing like that from Christ, if you have really heard his voice and understood the truth that Jesus has taught you. No, what you learned was to fling off the dirty clothes of the old way of living, which were rotted through and through with lust's illusions, and, with yourselves mentally and spiritually re-made, to put on the clean fresh clothes of the new life which was made by God's design for righteousness and the holiness which is no illusion.
>
> Finish, then, with lying and let each man tell his neighbour the truth, for we are all parts of the same body. If you are angry, be sure that it is not a sinful anger. Never go to bed angry—don't give the devil that sort of foothold. (Ephesians 4:17–27, PHILLIPS)

This passage is a reminder of the dramatic change possible in the Lord Jesus. So, instead of hiding away behind a file drawer full of theories of temperament (which have their basis not in the Bible but in pagan Greek thought), we must step up and fulfill our obligations. We ought to be aware that the changes God demands in His Word, He makes possible by His indwelling Spirit. After twenty-two years of marriage, I'm still trying to learn this lesson consistently—and to do this, I need the help and direction of good and godly friends who are able and willing to point out the blind spots I have developed over the years. As I see these blind spots and overcome them, the harmony described by Beth Nielsen Chapman and Eric Kaz in "All I Have" will characterize the marriage my wife and I share as we dwell together over a lifetime.

> *I feel like I've known you forever and ever*
> *Baby that's how close we are*
> *Right here with you is where my life has come together*
> *And where love has filled my heart.*
> *You know I'd go anywhere*
> *As long as I have you to care.*
>
> *All I have is all I need*
> *And it all comes down to you and me*
> *How far away this world becomes*
> *In the harbor of each other's arms.*

SACRIFICE

What have I done in the last seven days that was an act of sacrifice on my part for the sake of my spouse? This question has an uncomfortable way of confronting us with this crucial dimension of our marriages.

After almost fourteen years in America, I am increasingly fond of watching baseball. I know I do not appreciate all the "games within the game," but I understand the big picture. On certain occasions, players are asked to make sacrifices that will benefit the team. For example, one player might be instructed to bunt, which means he will probably be thrown out at first base. However, his "sacrifice" is likely to advance one or more teammates.

Sometimes we should "lay down a bunt" in marriage by choosing to ensure a spouse's advancement—regardless of the personal consequences. Indeed, the greatest joys in marriage ought to come out of the sacrifices husbands and wives make for each other. The giving up of myself for the well-being of my partner.

But when it comes to this we face a major problem—selfishness. Our sinful natures fight against the divine pattern that calls us to live for our partner and to meet his or her need of companionship and to find our greatest joy in seeing our spouse happy.

This challenge is further heightened by the fact that for the last twenty-five years psychological theory has been invading the church. Today, the Christian as well as the pagan has come to believe that "looking out for number one" is a cardinal tenet of mental wholeness. Indeed, what the apostle Paul describes as a disease (2 Timothy 3:2) is being heralded as a cure by those who ought to know better.

This preoccupation with self-esteem and self-love is nothing other than a gloss for selfishness. As we begin to meet with young couples who have been schooled in self-assertion and have grown up being constantly told they are "somebody" and "their own persons," it is increasingly difficult to bring them to an understanding of the nature of biblical marriage. They take this philosophy into the marriage, each one expecting to live as his or her own person and assuming that joint endeavors will be entered into on the basis of compromise.

This is a recipe for failure right from the start. Self-centered individuals who have had this tendency reinforced at church and at home will find it virtually impossible to transition to a marriage in which each is absolutely committed to putting the other first.

We can only in passing touch on one of the key passages used to teach the self-esteem theory. It emerges from a distorted exegesis of the words of Jesus in Matthew 22:37–40 when He was asked to identify the greatest commandment in the law. Quoting from Deuteronomy 6:5 and Leviticus 19:18, He said,

> "Love the Lord your God with all your heart and with all your soul and with all your mind." This is the first and greatest commandment. And the second is like it: "Love your neighbor as yourself."

Here, we are told today, there are three commands: love God, love your neighbor, and love yourself. Yet Jesus clearly says there are *two* great commandments. There is no command to love ourselves. Rather, the assumption underpinning the command to love our neighbors as ourselves is that we *already* love ourselves. So what are we to do? Obey the Bible!

The language of sacrifice is the stuff of missionary biographies, which are largely unread today. Jim Elliot understood the words of Jesus concerning losing one's life as a way of finding it: "He is no fool, who gives what he cannot keep, to gain what he cannot lose," he said. The route to a healthy self-image does not lie along the road of self-preoc-cupation but on that of self-forgetfulness.

Those who are tempted to pursue a good self-image will be destined to disappointment, while those who seek first the kingdom of God and His righteousness (see Matthew 6:33) will find that, as a by-product, they will not cherish exaggerated ideas of themselves but will gain a sane estimate of who and what they are under God.

Howard Hendricks gets to the heart of this when he writes:

> Many people are in love only with themselves. The smallest package in all the world is the person who is all wrapped up with himself. But in true love, a person thinks more of the happiness of others than he does of himself.
>
> If a young man can come into marriage with his paramount passion in life to completely satisfy his wife, and if the girl can come into marriage with her sole, exclusive purpose the satisfaction of her husband, and both are sold out to satisfying Jesus Christ, then you have the ingredients for an ideal Christian marriage.[3]

It is surely obvious from even a cursory reading of the marriage vows that they demand a signifi-cant level of self-renunciation. It is then up to the couple to discover how to put sacrifice into prac-tice on a daily basis. A husband may regard taking out the garbage as an act of sacrifice, but his wife may consider it merely his ongoing duty. He is deceived if he believes she is stirred by his magnanimous act of self-giving. She may be much more impressed when he puts down the large pile of work he took home in order to listen carefully and offer opinions on the wallpaper selections she has made. The more two people communicate, the better they will be at living sacrificially.

IMAGINATION

Imagination is a concept so frequently misinterpreted and misapplied that some people don't even want to consider its potential benefit. So first let's set some parameters to provide a proper context. When the Westminster Catechism asks the question, "What does the seventh commandment teach us?" part of the answer it provides is as follows:

> Since both our body and soul are a temple of the Holy Spirit, it is His will that we keep both pure and holy. Therefore He forbids all unchaste actions, gestures, words, thoughts, desires and whatever may excite another person to them.

This wise response clearly negates the contemporary nonsense about sexual fantasy being a useful means to marital harmony. Newspapers, magazines, and TV talk shows herald its normality and harmlessness, but we must be aware that it is a clear violation of biblical teaching. In this sense, fantasy reduces one's spouse to merely a mechanism for the fulfillment of lustful thoughts.

Job declared: "I made a covenant with my eyes not to look lustfully at a girl" (Job 31:1). Scripture records his words not only to demonstrate his commitment to righteousness, but also to set an example for us so we will follow in his steps. For some, this may go without saying. However, I have been asked even by couples on the threshold of marriage if it is all right to adopt the secular approach of fantasy to physical intimacy.

It is sad that we have allowed the secular media to define *imagination* in narrow terms of sexual fantasy. While seeking to avoid one extreme, we should beware lest we go off the scale on the other end. In contrast, I want to promote imagination at a much deeper level that affects the totality of marriage. I hope to debunk the notion that *righteous* is a synonym for *boring*. Healthy Christian marriages should be creative, daring, and occasionally extravagant.

It appears from observation and careful listening that many marriages are just plain dull. While routine in and of itself need not be boring, it is easy to fall into the trap of going through the motions again and again to the point of disinterest and disenchantment. If marriage reaches this low point, I believe in change for change's sake. It is in this sense that we need to use *imagination*. There ought to be a dynamism about what we are doing that allows us to experience the joy and thrill on a recurring basis.

In the early years of marriage, it isn't unusual to buy a card for your spouse and then sip on coffee, expressing just how jazzed you are by his or her friendship. You want to discuss how much you enjoyed your recent trip. You enjoy snuggling on the couch on a cold day. Is it maturity that brings an end to such displays of affection? I don't think so. Sadly, I think we get lazy and/or begin to take our life's partner for granted.

The creativity that marks courtship should not become a distant memory. Rather, we should cultivate creativity as an ongoing impetus for fresh expressions of love and devotion. I am not suggesting that a few superficial expressions of imagination, often promoted by self-interest, can make up for the absence of communication, carefulness, or hard work. But when those factors are in place, then imaginative acts of love can take a marriage to deeper and more meaningful levels.

It always causes me deep pain when a wife tells me how her husband has suddenly become

Mr. Imagination in pursuing another woman. Now she finds notes and cards and little gifts that he has bought for someone else. Now she discovers there is room for a companion, after all, on those evenings out of town. Now a lunchtime rendezvous is feasible, even though it had always been "most impractical" anytime she had suggested it. Abandoned wives always want to know, "Where was all that creativity while I was taking his shirts to the laundry, meeting him at the airport, and taking care of the kids while he was on business trips?"

As I work with such couples who desire repentance and reconciliation, it is often revealed that the wife has also been guilty of a lack of imagination. Of course, one must be careful to point such things out at the appropriate time and as graciously as possible. Lack of imagination is rarely the fault of only one partner in a marriage, though one spouse may be more blatantly "stuck in a rut" than the other.

If variety is the spice of life, we should all make a conscious attempt to keep our marriages interesting and break out of monotonous routines. Only when we get out of the rut will we be able to see how deep it was.

Marital failure is brought about by countless little decisions made daily that erode the relationship. But we can reverse the trend and use the same strategy for success by making countless small improvements over long periods of time. Just as the benefits of a savings account can only be appreciated after a lengthy period of time, it also takes a while to see the benefits of companionship, persistence, communication, and creativity within marriage. It will probably take most of us twenty-five years or more to feel the positive effects of marital "compound interest." And there are few rewards at that stage in life to compare with knowing you are closer to a spouse than you ever were before.

In the meantime, these "healthy marriage ingredients" of carefulness, endeavor, communication, sacrifice, and imagination must remain priorities —whether or not we sense immediate rewards for them. Plant them around your marriage as you would a hedge around your property. Paying attention to these principles will ensure that with God's help you will erect a barrier that will stand the test of time.

CONCLUSION

ondon's Heathrow Airport is one of the biggest and busiest in the world. The massive electronic information board updates itself every minute, announcing the arrival of flights from every conceivable part of the world and encouraging people not to miss their departures to all points of the compass. I usually sit there fascinated by the way in which air travel increasingly shrinks the world to a global village.

But this occasion was different. On previous occasions, I had made the journey to the States with heavy bags and a light heart. This time, I had only hand luggage, but a heavy heart. Usually when I go home to Great Britain, it is to speak at a conference or simply to enjoy a reunion with family and friends. But this visit was different. I was on a mission—a rescue mission! And now as I pondered all that had taken place in the previous forty-eight hours, I realized that only time would tell whether the venture had been a success or a failure.

The marriage of some dear friends was in grave danger. Years of plain sailing had been replaced with stormy waters, and they were drifting, rudderless, all the time taking on water and facing the awful prospect of shipwreck. While they had not yet run aground on the rocks, or been broken up by the fierceness of the storm, such a disaster appeared imminent.

What was it that accounted for their being so greatly off course? It certainly could not be attributed to poverty or to the absence of family or supportive friends. They were successful and attractive, with plenty of friends and lovely children —but they were drifting apart. As a homeowner might conceal a crack in the wall with a strategically placed painting, so they were managing to camouflage their condition from all but those who knew them best and loved them most.

I remember the first time I got an inkling of this. I was playing golf with a couple of friends. We were playing where the game was invented, and I am tempted to say how the game was intended to be played! In other words, we were walking, carrying our own bags, and enjoying the kind of conversation that is afforded by the absence of cart paths and electronic conveyance. My playing partner asked me if I had any material that would be useful in encouraging a work colleague who was showing an interest in spiritual things. "I'm sure I could come up with something that would be useful," I said, "but tell me more about the friend at work. What's led to this?"

And so my friend told me about a female worker who, on learning that he was a Christian, had approached him with some personal concerns. Scott had begun to try to answer her questions, and, in the course of time, she shared with him that her marriage was in shambles and made him privy to some of the details of her life that were not necessary for him to know. It was clear that she had confided in him to a degree that was actually unhelpful.

I seized the opportunity to pass on to my friend advice I had received some years before during my preparation for ministry. We had been warned about the dangers in pastoral ministry of involvement with women other than our wives. On one particular occasion, I remember an older minister saying quite forcibly to us that if there was a lady who appeared to be pursuing us for spiritual help, that we should "shunt her off to our wives, or to some other suitable female in the church." His use of railroad terminology helped to graphically convey the necessity of dealing quickly and forcefully with a potential for failure. It would be important, he said, to engage the help of a female in taking on the task of evangelism and discipleship. All kinds of dangers lurk down the other road, and, therefore, we should avoid it at all costs. In passing this advice on to my friend, I was aware that not only did he not think it was necessary information, but he was actually more than a little perturbed that I would even broach the subject with him.

In light of what you have just read, you will have identified the fact that the female involved had violated one of our principles, insofar as she was taking somebody of the opposite sex, other than her husband, into a domain that was really only her husband's to enjoy. My friend was failing to heed the warning that the individual who is so sure that he stands may be the one who is about to topple.

As we proceeded down the well-worn fairways and picked up our pace to beat the setting sun, we reminisced. He had been a teenager when I was called to my first pastoral charge. Sue and I had arrived, childless and eager to be an example and encouragement, especially to young people who were thinking about marriage and setting out on those early days of the journey. Scott and his girlfriend, Melanie, would often arrive at our front doorstep, looking for tea and advice. And there had been many an evening when, in a desire for our own privacy, we had sent them down the road without even a welcome.

However, I had enjoyed the privilege of marrying them and then watching as they became parents and established their home. When we had left for America in the eighties, we still kept in touch, and there had been various games of golf on both sides of the Atlantic in the years that had ensued. So, although we had been separated by an ocean and a good deal of time had passed, there was still a deep bond of affection and, on my part, a sense of genuine pastoral concern for both of them and their children. As we talked about how vitally important it was to remain true to our marriage vows, we even went so far as to agree that if ever either of us was to show signs of wavering, then the other would step in with a three wood and use it to shepherd the wanderer back on track!

I do not recall who won the game that day. Our rivalry on this occasion was overshadowed by this other more important matter. But with the game over, I paid no more attention to the incident. There was no reason to. I was just too skeptical, I told myself. I really need to learn to give people the benefit of the doubt. I would proceed on the basis that "no news is good news." But that maxim is only true sometimes. And this time it wasn't.

Why we had chosen to ask Melanie to get us some medication from Britain, I do not know. But when it arrived, it was accompanied by a note that essentially said, "I am afraid. Please help me." When Sue followed up by telephone, it became apparent that the concerns I had expressed on the golf course regarding the woman Scott had mentioned had not been ungrounded. Certainly my warnings had not been heeded. It was now clear that Scott had gotten himself emotionally entangled with this particular female.

The symptoms were very plain. A cooling of affection between Scott and Melanie. An increased absence from the home, especially in the evenings. Prolonged periods of inconsiderate treatment of the children, followed by bursts of almost manic creativity in responding to their needs. An unwillingness to engage in conversation with his wife. And, as it turned out, an unwillingness to receive the wounds, even of his friends.

I went into action, as if in response to a 911 call. I immediately sent a cryptic transatlantic fax to Scott, which read: "Remember what we said we would do if this ever happened!" I was to receive an equally cryptic response: "Message understood. Will be in touch."

I was not surprised when I never heard anything further. It would have been easy for me to convince myself that I was too long gone and too far removed to be able to do anything useful in these circumstances. But I found it impossible to "pass by on the other side." After all, we had promised one another, and a promise is a promise. No matter how hard it is to keep.

When after a number of attempts, I was finally able to talk with Scott on the phone, our conversation was marked, on his end, by evasion and superficiality. In the weeks and months that followed, the story just became worse. To some degree, both Scott and Melanie had begun to take each other for granted. They had settled into patterns of behavior that were not the best. Material success and career advancement were not enough to fill the holes that were becoming apparent in the fabric of their relationship. Scott had begun to compare his wife unfavorably with others. He was allowing himself a latitude with respect to his time, finances, and affections that was guaranteed to erode their marriage bonds. Sue and I kept in touch with Scott and Melanie as best we could, and we intervened from a distance, offering help, guidance, and correction, if and when they were prepared to receive it.

On one memorable occasion, Sue was awakened in the night with such a sense of heaviness on her heart in relationship to them both that she called their home in the early hours of the morning, only to discover that Scott had already packed his bags and had them at the doorway of the bedroom in prospect of leaving behind his wife and children and setting up in an apartment by himself.

I can remember waking out of sleep to hear Sue speaking in the most strident and certain tones to someone. As I gradually put the pieces together, I realized what was taking place. I marveled at her boldness and could only begin to imagine how surprised my friend was at the other end of the phone. He was used to a very demure and sensitive Sue, and had become accustomed to the forcefulness coming from my side.

But eventually it settled down to the standard pattern I have seen duplicated again and again throughout the last twenty years. Namely, two steps forward, one step back. All the same phrases trotted out, couched in the language of psychological theory. I was to listen again and again to classic expressions of self-interest.

Eventually, I could stand the distance no longer.

Sue and I agreed that I should make a journey back to Britain and at least have the opportunity to speak face-to-face with the two of them. We estimated that this would be as striking a way as any to convey our love and concern for them, and also the depth of feeling we had for each of their children, to whom we had actually become custodians in the event of the untimely passing of their parents. There was no other way I could adequately convey how much we cared, apart from getting on a plane and going to see them.

This was not a happy prospect for me. I was going, not so much out of a sense of desire as out of a commitment to duty. I could only assume that Scott would have done the same had the roles been reversed.

How else were we going to handle this but on the golf course? We were on the back nine before we got down to the real conversation. Let us allow a veil of silence to pass over the details of what was said. But let it be recorded that out there on that familiar grass, where our rivalry had been nurtured, where our laughter had filled the night air, we cried together and cried to God for His mercy and His grace. Back in the comfort of their lovely home, after we had enjoyed supper, the three of us knelt together and again asked God to do for us exceedingly abundantly beyond all that we could ask or even imagine.

And so I obeyed the Fasten Seat Belt sign, looked at my watch, and counted down the thirty-five or forty seconds from the time of hearing the 747's engines roar to feeling the wheels lift off the runway beneath me. And as the plane climbed above the clouds and headed north for Scotland before turning west over Ireland, I looked out the window and began to write to myself the notes that formed the substance of this book. I reflected on the fact that only the spirit of the Pharisee would pray at a time like this, "I thank you that I am not as other men are." And that the spirit with which one needed to pray was and remains, "God be merciful to me, a sinner." It was clear that "there but for the grace of God go any one of us." It was equally plain that there was no reason to presume upon our tomorrows. But, rather, there was an obvious call to a strident holiness and to a keeping of short accounts with anyone or anything that would draw us away from a zealous commitment to the wife or husband of our youth.

Through the months that followed, there were good days and bad days. Indeed, there were a number of days when it appeared that all of the affirmations on the golf course had gone by the way, and that the relationship would disintegrate once and for all. But as I write, Scott and Melanie and each of their children are together, happily so. They are involved in the ministry of a local church. They are establishing new patterns and friendships, while they are thankful for many of the old ones. They have resolved that the only way forward is forward. They have taken to heart Paul's words to the Philippians, so that, forgetting the things which are behind, they are pressing on "toward the goal to win the prize for which God has called [them] heavenward in Christ Jesus" (3:13–14).

They are a testimony to the healing power of God's grace and to what can take place when couples determine, with God's help, to channel their energies into reconciliation rather than using up their resources on finding imaginative ways to separate from one another and dissolve that which God has put together.

In over twenty years of pastoral ministry, I have not seen many situations come out in this way. Indeed, I could count them on one hand. In the vast majority of cases, circumstances such as I have just described have ended in disappointment and eventually divorce. My friends have graciously allowed me to include their story. It's not one they are proud of. It's not a journey they would have planned for themselves. But they recognize that, having been down those paths, they can be a help and an encouragement to others. Indeed, they can stand as a warning sign at various junctions, able to point out to others the foolishness of certain decisions—and at the same time, able to offer to them a helping hand on the journey to faithfulness and joy and the discovery that *love is not to be a victim of our emotions, but is to be a servant of our wills.* They serve as a reminder to us that with God, failure is never final.

NOTES

Introduction. What More Can Be Said About Marriage?

1. H. Norman Wright, *Seasons of a Marriage* (Ventura, Calif.: Gospel Light, Regal Books, 1982), 121.
2. Carl R. Rogers, *Becoming Partners: Marriage and Its Alternatives* (New York: Dell, 1973), 11.
3. Ben Hogan, quoted in *Hogan,* by Curt Sampson (Nashville: Rutledge Hill, 1996), 205.

Chapter 1. When Marriage Doesn't Go According to Plan

1. Jay E. Adams, *Solving Marriage Problems* (Grand Rapids: Baker, 1983), 24.
2. Ibid., 32.
3. "One Flesh," daily study for Wednesday, March 15, *Tabletalk* 19, no. 3 (1995):31. Reprinted from *Tabletalk* magazine with permission of Ligonier Ministries, P.O. Box 547500, Orlando, Florida 32854, 1-800-435-4343.

Chapter 2. Before We Say "I Do"

1. John Calvin, *The First Epistle of Paul the Apostle to the Corinthi-*

ans, trans. John W. Fraser, New Testament Commentaries, vol. 6 (Grand Rapids: Eerdmans, 1960), 159.

2. David Olsen, quoted in *Cosmopolitan,* May 1992.

3. Walter Wangerin, *Ragman: And Other Cries of Faith* (San Francisco: Harper San Francisco, 1994).

4. Jay E. Adams, *Solving Marriage Problems* (Grand Rapids: Baker, 1983), 34.

5. John R. W. Stott, *The Gospel and the End of Time: The Message of 1 & 2 Thessalonians* (Downers Grove, Ill.: InterVarsity, 1991), 84.

Chapter 3. Sealed with a Vow

1. Jay E. Adams, *Solving Marriage Problems* (Grand Rapids: Baker, 1983), 32.

2. Erma Bombeck, *A Marriage Made in Heaven* (New York: HarperCollins, 1993), 30.

3. Robertson McQuilken, "Muriel's Blessing," *Christianity Today,* 5 February 1996, 33–34. Used by permission of Robertson McQuilkin.

4. Hugh O'Neill and Greg Gutfeld, "Your Honey or Your Wife," *Men's Health,* January–February 1996, 72.

5. James H. Olthius, *I Pledge You My Troth* (New York: Harper & Row, 1975), 63.

6. Michael S. Horton, *The Law of Perfect Freedom* (Chicago: Moody, 1993), 180.

7. Jill Tweedie, *Guardian,* 1976.

8. Ibid.

9. Morton Hunt in Horton, *Law of Perfect Freedom.*

Chapter 4. The Role of a Wife

1. Felice Swartz, *Working Woman.*

2. John MacArthur, *Galatians,* The MacArthur New Testament Commentary (Chicago: Moody, 1987), 100.

3. Jay E. Adams, *Solving Marriage Problems* (Grand Rapids: Baker, 1983), 112.

4. Erma Bombeck, *At Wit's End* (Garden City, N.Y.: Doubleday, 1965, 1966, 1967), 13.

5. Jessie Bernard, *The Future of Marriage* (New Haven: Yale Univ. Press, 1982).

6. Walter J. Chantry, *The High Calling of Motherhood* (Carlisle, Pa.: Banner of Truth, n.d.). Used by permission of Banner of Truth.

7. Ibid.

8. Ibid.

Chapter 5. The Role of a Husband

1. Quoted by John MacArthur in *The Family* (Chicago: Moody, 1982), 95.

2. Tim Hansel, *What Kids Need Most in a Dad* (Old Tappan, N.J.: Revell, 1989), 29–31.

3. Chuck Swindoll, "Building Memories," *Moody,* April 1982, 28.

Chapter 6. Pulling Weeds

1. H. Norman Wright, *The Other Woman in Your Marriage* (Ventura, Calif.: Gospel Light, Regal Books, 1994), 138.

2. Jay E. Adams, *Solving Marriage Problems* (Grand Rapids: Baker, 1983), 76.

3. Wright, *Seasons of a Marriage,* (Gospel Light, Regal Books, 1982), 127.

4. Frank Pittman III,. quoted in Hugh O'Neill and Greg Gutfeld, "Your Honey or Your Wife, *Men's Health,* January–February, 1996.

5. John R. W. Stott, *Confess Your Sins* (Philadelphia: Westminster, 1964), 27.

6. Adams, *Solving Marriage Problems,* 77–78

7. Pittman, quoted in "Your Honey or Your Wife."

8. George Barna, *What Americans Believe* (Ventura, Calif.: Gospel Light, Regal Books, 1991), 83–85.

Chapter 7. Planting Hedges

1. Jay E. Adams, *Solving Marriage Problems* (Grand Rapids: Baker, 1983), 42.
2. Ibid., 39.
3. Howard Hendricks, "Yardsticks." Reprinted by permission of the author.

STUDY GUIDE
FOR SPOUSE AND
GROUP DISCUSSION

BY

JAMES S. BELL, JR.

To the Reader

In more than twenty years of pastoral ministry, Alistair Begg has worked with married couples who are struggling. Many of them know, at least in theory, what they need to do to make their relationship thrive, but don't have a plan to actually get the job done. The purpose of this study guide, then, is to take the excellent teaching and counseling based on years of experience from the author and "flesh it out" through application. The true evidence of success is not obtaining more knowledge of how to do the right principles in your marriage, but the transformed lives that result from actually performing them.

This guide is intended primarily for a husband and wife together, but can be utilized within a marriage group, small group, or adult Sunday school. Every couple will answer the questions and apply the material differently, according to their own experience and circumstances. Thus, sharing with other couples gives greater insight.

Do not feel guilty if you do not finish all the questions. Discuss those especially where you need to put in the most effort. You can profit from answering some of the questions in mere minutes. Others may take weeks or months before improvement is shown, but commitment to action is the key.

It is best to write down answers and record subsequent activity in a journal of some sort, either separate from your spouse or shared. The important criteria is progress, not instant transformation. This will provide an ongoing record of growth or lack thereof. Review these questions every six months or so to see if there is improvement. It is my hope that by your successful implementation of these principles, I will have helped the author realize the transformation in marriage that he so longs to see.

Introduction
What More Can Be Said About Marriage?

1. If you've read Christian marriage books in the past, list the major take-away value of your favorite ones. In what areas did they most benefit you? What issues did they not address or change in your marriage?

2. In what ways have psychological theory or other belief systems found in marriage books you've read perhaps subtly conflicted with God's Word? If not, have you substituted worldly teaching for a sound biblical grounding in marriage?

3. Refer to the story of the young professional and Elaine. At what level have you fallen into the same trap in the past through (a) discussing a spouse's shortcomings, (b) making mental comparisons, (c) spending time alone, and (d) physical intimacy?

4. What potential for the above dangers is possible in your present situation without the necessary safeguards?

5. Look at all the possibilities mentioned by Carl Rogers to substitute for the old-fashioned marriage. Think of friends and relatives who are using these methods. How are they working for them? What seems to be missing?

6. As with a good golf game, a few basic principles executed well make all the difference. What principles in your relationship with your spouse which you do on a regular basis are most successful?

7. A scripture reading for support and to identify with: Luke 14:28.

Chapter One
When Marriage Doesn't Go According to Plan

1. Review the opening story of Dave and Karen. Name three steps (in order) that Dave needs to take in relation to the two women in his life to save the marriage.

2. In the story of Cathy and Jack, what are Jack's options after hearing from Henry? What demands, sacrifices, or boundaries would you be willing to make under the circumstances?

3. When a marriage doesn't go according to plan, it's often because no plan has been clearly stated. Write a one-page plan that sets out your expectations, goals, and overall vision for your marriage as it relates to both partners.

4. In marriage we enter a covenant to be a helpmate and companion in every key area of life. Rate yourself from 1 to 10 in the following areas: sexual, social, intellectual, emotional, and spiritual. How might you improve your score in each of these critical areas?

5. Sarah displayed characteristics of a godly wife in Scripture. Locate one example each of a godly wife and husband in God's Word. How can you emulate their character in relation to their spouse? Suggested readings: Matthew 1–2; Luke 2 (Joseph and Mary); Acts 18:1–3, 18–19, 26 (Aquila and Priscilla). See also Ruth and Boaz (Ruth 1–4); and Hosea (Hosea 1–3).

6. List all the negatives the culture associates with a wife's submission to her husband. Now enumerate your own fears or dislikes. How does all of the above compare with the overall balance the Bible presents relating to the husband-wife relationship?

7. As seen in the *Tabletalk* quote, the marriage vows take into account all future problems, whether foreseen or not. This includes unemployment, disease, and old age. Frankly discuss all contingencies, hardships, and reversals and pledge your support in all circumstances.

8. Scripture for support and encouragement: Galatians 6:2.

Chapter Two
Before We Say "I Do"

1. Be completely honest with each other about past exploits, present beliefs, and behavior, as well as future plans and goals. Is there anything that you may be even subconsciously concealing that might have an impact on your marriage relationship? Discuss how this might affect each of you.

The following questions related to important traits in choosing a marriage partner alternate between husband and wife:

2a. Assess his present spiritual activities. Does his present spiritual walk measure up to the standards of a godly man?

2b. Does she have saving faith in Christ as both Savior and Lord of every area of her life? Does she trust His power and provision to meet every need?

3a. Does he walk with integrity in all his behavior and even attitude? Where does he fall short in the small things?

3b. Is she preoccupied with external beauty above the beauty of her character? Do her words and deeds have a continual lovely quality?

4a. Is he a resolute decision maker who carefully weighs options based on God's Word? Does he boldly accept consequences?

4b. Does she have the strong absolutes combined with initiative and faith to achieve joint goals? Is she willing to defer to the leading of her husband and support his judgments?

5a. Does he focus more on his own needs and feelings or those of others? How does he use his time, resources, and abilities?

5b. What do her words, heart, and attitude display to others? Is there anything that would embarrass her spouse rather than build confidence?

6a. Does he take himself or life too seriously, or do humor and joy fill his life? Does he indulge in the other extreme of sarcasm?

6b. Does she display kindness and gentleness starting with her children, or are there pockets of insensitivity and self-centeredness, perhaps with even a tinge of cynicism?

7a. Is his humility genuine by his concern for others and dependence upon God? How does he respond to his own achievements and failures?

7b. Can she maintain a positive, even humorous, attitude in the face of opposition and trial? Will she persevere and remain true even when things are tough without complaining?

7c. Make a list of other important traits and explore them in detail.

8. See Galatians 5:22–23 for godly characteristics that should be observed in each of us.

Chapter Three
Sealed with a Vow

1. Make a point of reading your original wedding vows. Have you done more or less to keep those vows, and what would it take to strengthen unkept (or neglected) vows?

2. Vow One: Have you both fully comprehended the meaning of marriage from a legal and spiritual standpoint? List the changes that occur as you relate spiritually, emotionally, and physically. Express your understanding of "cleaving" to your mate in an ongoing sense.

3. Vow Two: If marriage is God's *ordinance,* look up the meaning of that word as well as the word *covenant* to determine what God has commanded in terms of obligations. What circumstances will adversely affect or tempt you to modify this covenant? What are your chief barriers to intimacy?

4. Vow Three: Look at the key words *love, honor,* and *keep.* How can commitment replace emotion in the first case? What practical ways do we honor by putting the other first? Finally, in what areas can we look out for the other's interests?

5. Vow Four: Sickness can be devastating and require tremendous patience and a servant attitude. Discuss how you would respond to serious illness and what you would need from your own resources and from God to fulfill this vow. How have you learned by observing other marriages going through testing in this area?

6. Vow Five: Mental as well as physical infidelity are forbidden in marriage. Discuss your weaknesses due to unmet expectations or outside pressures. How can you establish the hedges that will protect you from all unfaithfulness, even that of the mind. See 1 Corinthians 10:13 for a Scripture verse to remember in times of temptation; see 1 Samuel 11:1–12:25; Psalm 51 for a warning of the consequences of yielding to temptation.

7. Vow Six: Separation and divorce are considered as options by some people even for general unhappiness. If you've ever considered these for any reason, make a pledge to surrender them as a negative option based on God's command, and agree to deal with the underlying issues leading in this direction.

Chapter Four
The Role of a Wife

1. Name some "supermodel" Christian women of today who exhibit attractive Christlike qualities. What are those qualities and why are they lovely? How can you emulate some of them in your life?

2. Submission and equality in marriage are not mutually exclusive. How can female assertiveness and initiative work well with male headship in your marriage? Where do adjustments need to be made by both partners to achieve the proper balance?

3. Recall a difficult situation or decision where you both strongly disagreed. How did you finally resolve it and on what principles? Based on the biblical concepts of submission and equality, would you do things differently were the same issues to come up today?

4. Many couples struggle with both proper male headship (both extremes), and appropriate female submission (both extremes again), but fail to realize that personality factors, upbringing, goals, etc., affect these imbalances. Examine and attempt to correct this in your present relationship.

5. Older women have a wealth of experience, both practical and spiritual, to utilize in coping with the stresses of being a wife and mother. Seek out an older, wiser Christian woman to share lessons she's learned, especially in your weak or difficult areas.

6. Lack of self-control can cause numerous problems in a marriage. Look especially at the areas mentioned by the author: finances, food, home, the tongue, and a pure mind and heart. Review these and add other areas of your life where you might not have balance or control. Take steps with the help of God and your spouse to improve.

7. Walter Chantry, in *The High Calling of Motherhood,* lists the main purposes of a mother's role in building strong character: developing talents, instilling virtues, correcting faults, and evangelizing. If you've missed or neglected one of these areas, set up a concrete plan to address it more thoroughly.

8. See 2 Peter 1:5–9 for godly qualities and virtues that should be evident in our lives.

Chapter Five
The Role of a Husband

1. List all your hobbies, recreation, friendships, etc., apart from work and family life. How much time, effort, and care go into each of them? Compare that total with the total investment in your wife. To put her first in your life, make plans, beginning with this month, to adjust your priorities.

2. Read together Ephesians 5:25–33. Now describe from the Gospels what Christ actually did for His church. Compare your attitude and actions by viewing your wife as representing the church. How can you become more Christlike in laying down your life?

3. Though our degree of love cannot equal Christ's, our attitude can reflect His character. How often does your love for your wife remain constant without expecting a response? Cite an example where you kept serving her without verbal affirmation.

4. At what times, due to your lack of commitment or ability, has your wife taken the role of leadership? How is this linked to your failure to first provide adequate love and attention to her needs? Discuss how you can regain the initiative.

5. Even when we demonstrate love, it's often only because it's convenient. What have you given up related to your own interests in order to love your wife and put her needs first? Sacrificial love is deliberate! Plan an event or action that will go the "extra mile" in her eyes because of the personal sacrifice involved. Read 1 Corinthians 13 for a description of true love.

6. In your training and instruction of your children, are you too directive, not allowing freedom or breathing room? Or are you nondirective, not providing them with clear guidelines in life? Pick a situation that demands a careful balance and take the proper steps.

7. Our most important task is teaching and training in the Christian faith. What have you done (or will do) to ensure that your children receive an understanding of Christian doctrine and how to apply it to their life situations? How can you and your wife also improve your prayer and fellowship time together and encourage each other in spiritual growth?

Chapter Six
Pulling Weeds

1. Past romantic relationships can come back to haunt us, especially at vulnerable times. Search your hearts for past sins of reliving desire or comparison with your present spouse. Confess to one another and resolve not only to eliminate this from your thought life but also potentially entangling circumstances or continuing relational ties. Read and memorize Scripture that emphasizes repentance, forgiveness, and putting the past behind. Suggestions: Luke 17:3; Ephesians 4:32; Philippians 3:13; 1 John 1:9.

2. If either spouse has children from a past marriage, those loyalties can also create many complications. In what ways have these other children and their needs impacted your own marriage relationship? How can you protect yourself from "old wounds" as well as keep both worlds within proper boundaries? What will you attempt to do to mend wounds and open doors to witness to these family members?

3. The issues related to your own children in your present marriage can become weeds that overrun your garden as well. Among the following, what are your chief areas of difficulty and what can you do to deal with the problem?

Infertility	Lack of desire for children
Lack of family planning	Their unmet expectations
The only thing holding you together	Discipline problems or approaches
Behavior a cause for diversion	Parental guilt for inadequacy

4. Sharing responsibilities (especially household) can be stressful when there are differing philosophies, time schedules, abilities, and interests. Look at these four considerations and write out general guidelines that will help your communication and daily decisions as you face daily domestic responsibilities.

5. We so take basic manners for granted that we often neglect them. As you serve each other, directly or indirectly, how often do you express gratitude, affection, compliments, or an explanation of why their service is meaningful and important to you? Assess your performance and come up with a rule of response for the future. Do you see areas needing improvement as your children observe and mimic you?

6. Comparison, even in small ways, saps the vitality from a marriage. Do you accept your spouse as he/she is at present or are you taking on the job of changing him/her? Take inventory of everything from physical characteristics to spiritual growth. Reaffirm your acceptance of your spouse, failures and all. Concentrate on the positives.

7. Past offenses, minor or major, from an unkind word to an affair, need to be confessed. This should be followed by true repentance, which should result in genuine forgiveness and healing. Without dredging up unnecessary past sins, confess those things that may be blocking a close relationship. Also confess bitterness and an ongoing lack of forgiveness. See James 5:16 for the value and necessity of this action.

Chapter Seven
Planting Hedges

1. On a piece of paper draw a series of levels representing different phases of your marriage. How well did you plan for past stages and what were the results? How are you doing in your present stage? What will be the challenges of the future as you face challenges such as college, weddings, and retirement? Try to identify some possible challenges you hadn't thought about and address them thoroughly.

2. Similar to the author, we all have our blind spots, even if we've been married over twenty years, and our mates see them clearly. Even if you've heard about them previously, lovingly discuss each other's weaknesses that may not be apparent or fixable. List progressive steps in which you can help your mate change, without rejecting or criticizing him/her.

3. The language of sacrifice permeates the lives of the saints through the centuries. With your spouse, choose a favorite book on this subject, and after reading it together, outline the principles of sacrifice that apply to your marriage. As with Jim Elliot, find two or three memorable quotes that you will use in terms of servanthood, and make a note of the qualities in their lives that you admire.

4. Did you truly come into your marriage with a passion to completely serve and satisfy your spouse? If you had to lose everything else—career, hobbies, dreams—to merely serve your spouse's needs, would you be willing to do it? How have you succeeded at this task compared to your other goals and desires in life?

5. What are your most difficult challenges in serving or communicating with your wife? Generally, these challenges revolve around times when your favorite or most critical activities coincide with those you least like related to your spouse's needs. Try to isolate these. Think of three ways in which you can please each other daily, and do them. Ask each other "What can I do to serve you?" The requests may be the same for years, or they may change weekly.

6. Has your marriage seen dull patches? This is normal, but disinterest and disenchantment should not be allowed to settle in. What effect has routine or monotony (perhaps with stress added) had upon your marriage? What exciting things can you plan to counterbalance these inevitable dull patches?

7. "Compound interest," or the cumulative effects of what is continually positive about your marriage, is one of the greatest benefits of a long relationship. What investments of companionship, creativity, etc., are paying off exponentially?

Conclusion

1. Similar to the author, make a pact with a friend of the same sex regarding purity and sexual fidelity to your spouse. Agree to share and ask questions regarding the details of relationships with members of the opposite sex apart from your spouse. Memorize a verse to recall in times of challenge. Recommendation: 1 Corinthians 10:13.

2. Do you know of any couples who may benefit from your joint interest in their marriage? What can you both do to get involved and provide support and accountability? Take the first step and pray that your godly precepts can make a difference in helping them to shape their own pure and vibrant marriage.

3. Make it a priority to be involved with other couples on a regular basis, in order to support and be accountable to one another in your marriage relationships. Church small groups and Sunday schools are ideal (Hebrews 10:25).

Another Great Title from Alistair Begg and Moody Press

Made for His Pleasure

Ten Benchmarks for a Vital Faith

The prayer that pleases God is larger than ourselves. It focuses on the glory of God and remembers the needs of others. The life that is truly fulfilling gives back to God the talents and abilities He has given us to be used for His glory.

Alistair Begg applies these principles to ten areas of our lives and challenges us to experience our Father's pleasure as we glorify Him.

"A book by Alistair Begg—What a welcomed arrival! What he's done through his pulpit, he now offers through his pen: delightful, insightful teaching of God's Word. May this book be the flagship of a fleet to follow."
Max Lucado

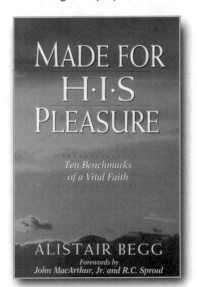

"This book from the pen of Alistair Begg is a chronicle of his own spiritual pilgrimage. It reads as a spiritual road map, a trustworthy guide to vital faith and life."
R.C. Sproul

ISBN: 0-8024-7138-2

MOODY
The Name You Can Trust
1-800-678-8812 **www.MoodyPress.org**